Existential Encounters

Other books by the same author

General Psychology
Hypnosis-A Clinical Study
A Coat Of Many Colours

Existential Encounters

S. Sunder Das

iUniverse, Inc.
New York Lincoln Shanghai

Existential Encounters

iUniverse, Inc.

For information address:
iUniverse, Inc.
2021 Pine Lake Road, Suite 100
Lincoln, NE 68512
www.iuniverse.com

ISBN: 0-595-29438-3

Printed in the United States of America

To My Wife Santha

Contents

Introduction

There are two sections in this book. The first deals with a special type of psychotherapy, which I have termed Broad Spectrum Psychotherapy. It describes an existential method to cope with the problems of life, some pathological and some that occur in the natural course of events. Case studies have been provided to illustrate the methods adumbrated. I have to say that it is a novel method devised during my forty odd years as a practising Clinical Psychologist both in India and Australia. During my professional life only one Psychiatrist has been kind enough to try this method and to inform me that it works. I have found that many of my fellow psychologists have not thought fit to give it even a cursory trial. I have no quarrel with them at all. The have chosen the easy method of conforming to the methods they have learned during their training. As far as the contents of this book are concerned, if some parts of it seem complicated and difficult to understand, I can only say in my defence that existential writing can sometimes be that way because of the concepts involved. But if the reader would persevere, things might get clear.

The second section, which I have termed Gallimaufry, contains a collection of articles dealing with problems of everyday life which one encounters in this world. The Chambers dictionary defines this word as a miscellaneous gathering or any inconsistent or absurd medley. I plead guilty to both. It is an exercise in thinking aloud. All these articles deal with the problems of this world. We can make it a more beautiful place to live in, if we only tried.

Prologue

Anything that is written on the topic of living tends to be looked upon by both therapists and laymen as philosophical in nature and therefore to make for "heavy" reading. These two charges cannot be immediately refuted for there is a great measure of truth in them. Nevertheless, philosophy in its simplest form means only the pursuit of knowledge and wisdom. As human organisms live and have their being on this earth, the existential study is an attempt at analysis of their modes of living and could be seen to be of vital importance to everyone. There is no ready answer to the second charge. Writings on life will continue to be involved and complex in that they have to try to grapple with problems of ontology. Meaning, its levels and distortions become important in as much as they deal with changes in one's perception of oneself in relation to others. Most modern languages, including the English tongue, can express ontological concepts only using their vocabularies in a unique manner. Despite the presence of a specialised terminology in literature dealing with such topics, mere mastery of words seems inadequate in the struggle to understand what the writer tries to say.

All therapists come across human beings referred to them as patients for treatment and assessment. In every case, the problems are presented as being desperate and needing urgent solution. This is the viewpoint of the patient. The therapist, on the other hand, in his own d need to evolve some order out of the chaos, labels some emotional ills as being desperate, others as being mild, some requiring urgent, active treatment and others as being able to wait for a little while. For the experiencing human being every problem is desperately urgent. This is not to deny that there are many people referred to as being mature and who can live with problems of an insistent nature for many years without coming to the crisis situation. Some of these people have experienced their difficulties fully, studied them adequately and sought for solutions consistently before keeping them in abeyance. This can perhaps be looked at as the establishment of right priorities. There are other people, who having had a fleeting glimpse of a problem looming large in their horizon, have thrust its recognition completely out of awareness, refusing the accept its reality. The problem thus becomes a gnawing pain, in that its non-recognition by banishment from full awareness does not mean its eradication. It only goes underground whence it exercises a deleterious effect on the person's existence. This seems like Freudian repression in its mechanism. Perhaps the resemblance is only in its aetiology. In the thesis presented in this book, non-awareness has been seen as device for the reduction of sampling of experiential modes. As such it is seen as a decimation of the gestalt and a return to atomistic modes of living. Life then becomes a pursuit of pleasure and the deliberate avoidance of pain. Sampling of only one area of existence is seen as a denial of authentic organismic behaviour, which seems to go by contrasts. Predominant occupation with pleasure also results in satiation and dependence on external events to overcome loneliness and boredom. It is implied in this thesis that man in his holistic nature is built for existing alone in the midst of many others as also for being with others. It thus follows that man cannot legitimately look upon external sources for the pursuit of his self-actualising needs. If he is the microcosm he must have within himself a miniature representation of the macrocosm and he should look within for a fuller life. Dependence on vicarious experience as a valid existential mode has been questioned in this book. Man perhaps needs to stress individuality. The development of cultures, which claim to be modern in their approach to life, all seem to emphasise the levelling aspects of togetherness and not its individuating characteristics.

Concepts such as love, suffering and death, which are normally avoided by people because of their being too intense and too close to unpleasant realities form the cornerstone of existential approaches. This is not because the existential approach considers itself as having transcended essential human experiences. It is only that the process of deliberate focussing of attention away from certain realities is not considered adaptive to the human organism. In the Western world the existentialists have been accused of being pessimistic and of emphasising suffering as the means of restoring meaning to life.

In Eastern ways of life, most of which are existential approaches, there is an important difference in conceptualisation. Suffering and pain as such, are considered to have no intrinsic value by themselves in creating or sustaining meaning to life. They are referential experiences which seem to sharpen perceptual systems as well as experiences of happiness only because our nervous system seems to operate in that fashion; that is, contrasting states of physical being seem to make for healthy functioning of the human organism. The whole of this small volume can therefore be seen as a comparison of views and cultures. This is to enable the reader to appreciate some of the differences that do occur while living amongst the different peoples of the world. Some of the less known systems of therapy have been touched upon briefly and case studies given to illustrate them.

The thesis developed in this book attempts some economy together with simplicity in postulating a holistic aspect of Love rather than innumerable love-relationships in day-to-day life of the human being. The seeming differences in relationships have been postulated as being due to differential emphases amongst the constituents of the love relationships, which last remain the same in their composition. Sudden changes in polarity of attitudes as also other changes in love-relationships can be adequately explained inside the framework of this theory.

Categorisation and labelling have been considered as of prime importance in man's experiences, not because these create order but because these can sometimes bring into being barriers imprisoning the organism and smothering it with conformity. Existential systems therefore aim at three important aspects; first by the creation of the awareness of the fetters (frames of reference), second by the facilitation of movement outside the radii and third the transcendence over the "ought-nature" of rules of behaviour.

As with all gestalt systems, the theme developed in this book also underlines a very important aspect, namely that day-to-day living and the role of the therapist in restoring emotional serenity to the client are not two separate things. Not only are these two inter-related in an intimate sort of way but they are also based on compatible and similar principles. In other words both consist of strategies, their creation and their application. Both deal with repetition of successful modes and the relinquishing of unsuccessful ones. Both emphasise the unfolding of awareness and of learning patterns. In both, the human organism comes into contact with the intense joys and distress of love-relationships. As such it is futile perhaps to talk of *a* successful life or *the* successful life. The only successful life is perhaps one, which is evolutionary as regards the aspects referred to above.

Another important aspect also needs to be looked at. In the usual interaction between the client and the therapist, whatever their persuasions, the final goal is set out as the achievement of adequacy in daily living by the client. This means that the therapy ceases soon after both parties perceive that the client has acquired confidence as also some adaptive strategies, which would enable him to function at a tolerable level of adequacy. This is a good thing in that any dependency feeling on the part of the client is broken and he is enabled to develop feelings of responsibility for his own behaviour. The disadvantage, seen at the completion of conventional psychotherapy is that both the client and the therapist seem to believe in the maintenance of a certain level of stability by the former. This sets a limit on the self-actualisation process. In other words the client is expected to be satisfied with his post-therapeutic behaviour patterns. In existential therapy there need not be a clear-cut distinction between the active therapeutic sessions in which the client and the therapist take part, and the sallies into life, which the client undertakes on his own. The processes of self-awareness and adaptiveness established during the first phase have to continue to evolve if the client is not to give up striving. This book therefore looks at possibilities for continued unfolding of awareness, the plausibility of increasing the conscious experiences while depleting the unconscious and the necessity of sampling all areas of existence irrespective of whether they are pleasurable or distressing.

In the savouring of existence in the fullest possible manner, the experience of love and the anticipation of death, remain the two most meaningful experiences. Love has been conceived of as a gestalt phenomenon, which transcends but includes aspects of sexual activity. Exercises designed to initiate the experience of as many constituents of the love-gestalt as possible, have been outlined. The experience of death as also its anticipation have been seen not as terrifying prospects looming in the horizon. The being-for-death, in other words the constant readiness for death, robs it of its terrifying power. The controversy amongst existentialists to the meaningful connection between life and death has been deal with.

Finally, this book has no pretensions as to the provision of answers for the host of problems, which assail the human being. All that it sets out to do is to formulate a holistic theory of love, which is seen as the greatest human experience. Wars, phobias and mental malaise can perhaps be explained as the failure to apprehend this very special aspect of love.

SECTION ONE

—

BROAD SPECTRUM
PSYCHOTHERAPY

A Concept of Love

Psychologists have always wondered as to whether or not the capacity to love others is innate in the human organism. In other words, is the love response something that exists before the evidence of learning? This has been and continues to be a difficult question to answer. Studies in this field have been complicated by the fact that responsible man has always considered human life as sacrosanct and therefore not to be subjected to experimental studies if these entail any deliberate deprivation, physical or psychological.

When a human baby is reared in a reasonably warm, "normal" home, its ontogenic development is characterised at first by emotional transactions with the parents and siblings if any, then with other significant human beings in its immediate environment and finally as an adult, with strangers as well. This consummation, which makes for an adult ready to deal with other human beings without a great deal of preconceived notions about them and without undue prejudice or hatred, is known as "a healthy development". This concept is again a relative one–people occupying various rungs in this ladder and differing in the degree of development in this area.

A second aspect concerns differentiation. Most workers with children seem to agree that for the infant the environment and its own self form a conglomerate in which the self is not differentiated from the non-self. Learning to see the self as distinct from the environment is also a gradually evolving character. For a young child, this could lead to all kinds of complications. His own phantasy life, for instance, is not properly distinguished from events "out there" with the result that thinking acquires a magical quality. Thus a child, by an act of will, can transform someone whom he dislikes into an animal; he can invent a fairy godmother who takes away all his misery. To an adult these seem merely imaginary exercises but to a child these are much more than exercises because he believes in the reality of his creations. In a wholesome pattern of ontogenetic development, the first clear-cut distinction is the one that occurs between him/her and the environment. The fact that this separation has occurred does not necessarily mean that the experiencer is a differentiated individual. Inside of him there are a number of attributes that initially exert their effect in a global fashion. A person undergoing the gradual process of differentiation becomes aware of every one of these attributes, in turn. Once maximal awareness has taken place, the attribute in question is perceived as partly autonomous. This does not mean that the attribute acquires functional autonomy expressing itself without the experiencer's volition or awareness. It only means that a great extent of spontaneity has been generated in relation to it and that no rigidity or conformity holds the experiencer back. In other words inhibition and conformity have been transcended. Personality differentiation is said to have taken place maximally when most of the attributes have been felt in awareness as having clear-cut specialised functions and therefore as being capable of expression individually without guilt or inhibition. Contrary to the expectation of many therapists and clients alike, this stage of differentiation is not seen by the existential psychologist as the highest form of evolution. Perhaps there are higher stages too. The next ascending stage in the evolutionary phase is the development of awareness of the unity amongst these attributes and of the influence of every one of these in the total expression of the personality. A person who has attained this stage is said to be integrated. The essential difference between a new born baby whose personality also expresses itself in a global fashion and the integrated person consists in that the latter has maximal awareness of his personality attributes, the way in which each of these elements can express itself autonomously and finally how these combine together to exert their influence to produce a myriad of rich experiences. To sum this up, ontogenetic evolution follows first a pattern of differentiation of the individual personality and then results in the total integration of the human organism.

It would therefore seem obvious that differentiation and integration being the essential attributes of an evolving human individual, the position of any person can be located on a continuum, the lowest end of which represents non-differentiation and the top end, integration. A concept implicit in this formulation is that whereas differentiation can exist in the absence of adequate integration, the latter cannot exist without an individual having gone through the experience of differentiation. The foregoing concepts, while clarifying the possible stages of ontogenetic personality development are not meant to carry any self-limiting connotation, namely that integration is the height of self-actualisation a person can achieve. Integration itself can be seen as a continuum having a lower point. The upper end of the continuum can be considered as an abstraction as we have no way of gauging the limit of this evolution.

Differentiation assists in reality-orientation and clearer perception of reality. This is because it represents a stage of better demarcation, not only amongst the attributes of the self but also between the self and the environment. Greater facilitation in the perception of reality is synonymous with increase in awareness. There are specific ways in which the human personality is expressed. Love may be considered the most important of these, because in the existential sense it determines a person's behaviour pattern in relation to other people in his world. All human beings are preoccupied with thought of whom they should love or hate, how they are to do this, and whether these stances would result in acceptance or rejection. They are also occupied with thoughts of how the expression and the receiving of love can result in increase of self-esteem whereas non-receipt of love can plunge them into a gloom of self-pity and self-denunciation. All human beings experience and need love-relationships. But the concept of "love" is a much-maligned one, meaning different things to different people. Most of the meanings given to love are restricted ones denoting only some aspects of it especially because human beings persist in classifying love-relationships into innumerable categories. In the English language and indeed in most other languages there are innumerable expressions like tenderness, affection, regard, compassion, concern and caring (to quote just a few) which seem to convey qualities of love. One of the things that most people believe is that any one of these qualities can be expressed by itself without the others exerting their influence. Based on this belief, people try to set up love relationships seemingly characterised by just one or more of the above qualities. The thesis put forward in this book is for the existence of just one holistic love pattern including all the innumerable qualities that people ascribe to it. This holistic love will be termed the Love-Gestalt. It is also postulated here that there is only one kind of love in all human relationships namely the Love-Gestalt. The question immediately arises as to how, if there is only one kind of love, we can explain the seemingly myriad patterns of love-relationships seen in human lives. A further concept needs to be clarified to understand this seeming paradox. That is the concept of emphasis. The love-Gestalt, the only kind of love possible in all human relationships can be seen as compounded of all the qualities that human beings ascribe to love. Due to cultural conditioning the young child quite early in life, learns to emphasise some qualities of the Love-Gestalt in every human love relationship. This means that some qualities of the Love-Gestalt receive greater attention and awareness in every such relationship. It may thus been seen that in the love a child has towards its mother, the quality of tenderness may have been treated as most important. The same child in its love relationship towards its father would emphasise the quality of admiration. In other words, the love of a father towards a child, that of a child towards its mother, that of a wife towards her husband and that between friends can all be seen as qualitatively the same Love-Gestalt but differing only in the particular quality that has been emphasised. It becomes also possible to see how great an influence the culture of any society can play in the development of appropriate emphases in human relationships. Take the concept of incest for example. Amongst the ancient Egyptian Pharaohs it was customary for a brother to marry his sister. This love relationship was not considered incestuous although a common Egyptian of those days knew that he could not marry his own sister because he would feel incestuous. So within the same society contemporaneously, people in different social strata learned to emphasise different qualities in the same love-relationship.

In some societies they do not have an equivalent word for "cousin" because a cousin in such societies is considered a brother or sister as the case might be. Among such people, a marriage between cousins or sexual attraction between them is taboo. Should such a love-relationship arise in that society the mode of address "brother" which a girl directs towards her cousin, is itself the source of confusion and trauma. The word "brother" defines some love emphases, which be inappropriate if directed towards a person to whom a girl has a sexual attraction. Here the need to emphasise a particular quality of the love-gestalt conflicts with emphases established by custom and semantic usage.

Another example would be that of a boy and girl who grow up as friends participating in study and games emphasising the caring aspect of their Love-Gestalt. Their schooldays could perhaps pass without any change in emphasis of the love-gestalt. Then suddenly one day without any volition on their part, they fall in love. This phenomenon is very difficult to explain other than by postulating a change in emphasis, which occurs suddenly. This is a very common human experience.

One of the basic assumptions made here is that all intact human organisms have felt the need for approach behaviour towards others. Another is that all human beings have the capacity to experience all the types of love relationships known to man. Some explanation is needed as to why many people seem unable to undergo the experience of different types of love-relationships. What restricts them may be their non-awareness of two aspects, first that love is a gestalt and secondly that love-relationships differ only in terms of emphasis. If there is a shutting out of significant aspects love and the consequent impoverishment of experiential modes it would be expected that such an experiencer would find himself severely restricted in love relationships. In brief, the positive emotional valence expressed in interpersonal relationships, to be considered adaptive and satisfying should perhaps fulfil the following two conditions:-

1. The experiencer should become aware progressively of more and more components represented in the love-gestalt.

2. His love-relationships should reflect the appropriate emphases. The failure to discriminate among these emphases represents a lack of differentiation as also of integration.

The "Negative" Emotions:-

One implication of the thesis developed here is that bipolarity of emotional patterns need be accepted only as a semantic differential and as necessarily having an objective or discernible existence. In other words experiential modes seem to demonstrate that satisfying growths of personality result from exercises in the expression of love, which can be seen as an approach or positive valence in interpersonal relationships. It is commonly seen that human beings do express hatred, anger and other "negative" emotions at times. The expression of these is readily seen to retard the growth of the organism in a subtle psychophysiological manner. Psychosomatic investigations have established that the experience of continuing anger, hatred and fear can affect the physiological functioning of the human organism in deleterious ways, often resulting in irreversible histological damage. These findings seem to lead us to the inference that the human body, without which our experiential modes cannot be savoured on this earth, has been geared to express some aspects of our emotional life not only with impunity but also with concomitant growth patterns and that it can express some others only with damage to itself. Taking all these into account, it seems possible to talk of positive and negative aspects of existential expression, this dichotomy based purely on the results an emotion has on the organism. Hatred is thus seen as the negative expression of love. Although philosophically some writers have denied the objective existence of hatred, the thesis presented here could avoid any metaphysical implications by merely viewing hatred as a maladaptive aspect of existential expression and by viewing love as an adaptive aspect judging by its growth aspects on the organism. It is also possible to look upon adaptive expressions as having the capacity to extend experiential modes thereby enriching all mentations whereas non-adaptive expressions may be seen to have an inhibitory effect on experience and therefore to lead to impoverishment of mentation. In this sense love may be said to disinhibit the personality of man and hatred to inhibit it. Any such inhibition in turn can be seen to lead to feelings of emptiness, which is one of the main problems of this technocratic age.

Anger is another emotion with similar inhibitory characteristics. Sometimes ethologists have observed aggressive behaviour not directly expressed towards the legitimate stimulus object but resulting in displacement activity. This has been observed mainly in sub-human organisms. These tend to occur especially when there is ambivalence consequent on the simultaneous arousal of two incompatible drives existing at near equal intensities. The adaptive value of such displacement seems to be the insurance of the continued survival of the species. In the case of the human being, most displacement seems to be shrouded in sophisticated or subtle behaviour patterns not readily amenable to being teased out easily.

In a sense, anger and hatred have become ubiquitous and are even encouraged as a means of displacing other existential frustrations. One has only to look at the experiential patterns of peoples and nations, which have overcome the problems of hunger, poverty and physical deprivations by increasing their wealth. Still despite affluence, the problems of boredom, of loneliness and of diminishing identity with the human experience as a whole, assail the people of such societies. These can be referred to as core problems because mental health depends on their successful resolution. At the moment affluent nations with such problems find it necessary to embark upon bellicose activities outside their own territories to erase the problems of emptiness. Such extra-territorial adventures are often rationalised as being the championing of just causes of oppressed peoples. This is not a value judgment but only an emphasis on the fact that man's displacement activities have veered away from their adaptive implications and seem directed towards the decimation of other human beings. In terms of the thesis put forward here, displacement activities result because of non-awareness of the love gestalt. There is a choice that every human has to make sometime or the other in his life and perhaps to continue to do so throughout his life. The choice is between an expanding awareness resulting from experiencing the love-gestalt progressively, with attendant pain, or reduced awareness with a sharp diminution of pain. No mystical or compensatory principle is involved when one speaks of pain resulting from greater awareness. With increasing awareness comes increased sensitivity and therefore the keener perception of pleasure as also pain. With reduced awareness goes reduced sensitivity and diminished perception of pleasure and pain. In the latter case diminished pain seem a desirable state of affairs but it would not be considered so when one realises that diminution of pain has been achieved at the expense of experiential modes. In other words avoidance of pain has been accomplished by paying a price, namely the telescoping of the range of experiences.

In summary, one of the important ways in which human existence can be expressed is in terms of love. The thesis advanced here looks upon love as a holistic entity referred to as the Love-Gestalt. All love that human beings express is seen to be the same. The Love-Gestalt itself seen as a holistic manifestation of love has very many attributes or qualities which one becomes aware of in a gradually increasing degree. The myriad love patterns that human beings think they express are not seen as essentially different love-relationships but the same Love-Gestalt with differential emphasis of one or more of its components. It has been implied that changes in emphasis are possible and a seemingly different type of love-relationship can emerge. The striving of man is seen to be towards greater awareness of the gestalt nature of love and towards apprehension of more and more qualities of the Love-Gestalt. The evolving man also seeks to distinguish among the range of emphases possible and their appropriateness in different human relationships. This learning process is a function of the culture in which that human being has his/her being. So within that particular cultural framework, there are norms for appropriate emphases. Human beings exhibit growth patterns when the love-gestalt is appropriately expressed. The concept of reality has been considered a consequence of the growth pattern. Damage to the organism—physical or psychological or spiritual—has been considered a consequence of the pursuit of unreality. Reality and unreality have been seen as functions of greater awareness and less awareness respectively. These do not have the same connotations that psychiatrists imply when referring to neuroses and psychoses. It has been accepted that human emotions tend to be bipolar. The growth end of this continuum has been considered positive and real, whereas anything that stands for restriction in growth patterns has been seen as negative as also unreal. Hatred and anger belong to the latter. Without making moral judgments or evaluations it has been hypothesised that awareness of and practice in the expression of the Love-Gestalt would lead to an experientially richer existence. It may also be hypothesised that with greater degrees of self-actualisation, the seemingly different types of love-relationships will give way to gestalt love, which results in equal emphasis of most of the attributes.

By an extension of this idea it is possible to postulate that maximum self-actualisation can be said to have been achieved when a human being can experience love, which expresses equal emphases among all its constituent elements. Then there will be only one kind of love. Agape the ultimate in Christian love is an example of this.

Culture And The Human Organism

Circumstances do not always favour the human being. The need to create ecological harmony, the clamouring internal need for homeostatic balance, the drive for preserving one's self-esteem while respecting the other's requirement for achievement and the ability to maximise one's potentialities are some of the very complex and not altogether compatible tasks confronting a sophisticated man. The question is, where he should start. How is he to establish priorities? Which ideologies should he espouse? Should he operate within his cultural norms or try to transcend them? Is it humanly possible to be broadminded? In other words, can a human being be non-aligned adopting attitudes according to the merits of the circumstance in which he finds himself? These and a host of existential questions have been asked since man learned to live within self-governing groups of his own kind. These questions will continue to be asked in the future too. The trouble is not these questions cannot receive answers but that the answers do not seem to have universal application. These could apply to a large number of people within any given culture but it is doubtful that the members of disparate cultures could find any measure of transcultural agreement in the answers they find. Cultural differences are therefore not myths but meaningfully disparate patterns of behaviour, which most careful observers could categorise under specific heads.

There are many ways in which a study like the one referred to above could be attempted. A few representative cultures could be analysed to bring out the salient differences, varying in degrees of intensity. It seems to the writer that this attempt is too difficult and ambitious a task. It is proposed therefore to postulate two "extreme cultures" which perhaps do not really exist in their pure form as represented here; nevertheless it may help to bring many transcultural differences under a meaningful dichotomy. The two extreme cultures can be delineated as the Western and the Eastern ones. These are to occupy the ends of a continuum along which the behaviour characteristics of any human being can be located. The extreme Eastern culture would then represent all the human characteristics referred as being particularly Eastern on non-European. The other end of the continuum would then represent the culture of the Western nations, which consider themselves technologically advanced societies. It would immediately become apparent that not all "Eastern" nations would have similar cultures. Nor will all Western nations have similar Western cultures. The ends of the continuum would only represent hypothetically "pure" types.

The first essential difference between the cultures lies in the concept of normality. Personality profiles can be looked at in many ways, one of the simplest and economic systems of classification being the dichotomy into Introverted and Extraverted types. While keeping the Jungian characteristics of these personality types as reference points, the writer wishes to analyse these in terms of the empirical differences in learning, performance and thinking patterns. The "normal" person in the West is the extraverted one with outgoing interests and with emphasis on the overt expression of behavioural patterns. Therefore, physical activities like sport and games should merit a great deal of attention in such a culture. In the East, the habit of looking within has been emphasised over many centuries resulting in the cultural norm of the introverted person. The genetic predisposition, which some psychologists subsume for patterns of introversion and extraversion, is perhaps difficult to prove or disprove, but it seems that socialisation processes emphasising the life of any community could make for the individual with these values.

The concept of the real and unreal also seems to be inextricably interwoven with the patterns of introversion and extraversion. In the West, with its emphasis on the tangible as the real, it is but natural that anything that cannot be apprehended by the senses tends to be considered as being superstitious and unscientific. By contrast, in the East the phenomenological world of the intangible receives the most attention and is seen as the real one. Cultural and intellectual pursuits would then be seen to follow differential patterns depending on the concepts of reality. In the realm of mental health also this has an important implication. It would be expected for instance in psychotic illnesses which manifest the alienation from reality, the schizophrenic in the East would show cultural patterns approximating to the normal in the West and vice-versa.

The writer has observed young married schizophrenic women in India and a comparable patient population in Australia. In India, where women do not normally discuss sexual matters with men, schizophrenic women have been seen to describe to the therapist in great detail their intimate sexual relationships with their husbands. It has also been seen that their natural inhibition in this regard would come into effect as they reverted to "cultural normality" (cure?). In Australia a comparable sample of schizophrenic women has been seen to be unusually reticent in talking about their sexual experiences. When they become better, their normal disinhibitory processes were seen to assert themselves. In both cases we could postulate the operation of an inhibitory process represented by the schizophrenic illness. In the former case the inhibitory process acts on the existent cultural inhibitory pattern thereby removing the inhibition. In the latter, the schizophrenic process inhibits an existent freedom from inhibition.

And stemming from habits of looking within or without, arise doctrines of Negation and Affirmation respectively. The doctrine of Negation can be described as a way of life characterised by a single-minded search for the essence of existence, negating or not paying attention to incidental phenomena not relevant to the quest. Affirmation refers to the savouring and the emphasising of experiences seen as pleasant and wholesome to the organism. In many Eastern philosophies there is the emphasis on eschewing Maya which consists of tangible manifestations of phenomena considered as illusory and therefore of being secondary in importance. Most Western cultures teach their members to affirm and label observable phenomena. These differences are readily seen amongst the students of a culture residing in countries having the "opposite' culture. The Eastern student seems to place undue emphasis on his learning to the exclusion of everything else, while his western counterpart takes part in a number of activities, which may not be of direct relevance to his studies. Public schools and well-known Universities in Britain, for instance, go to enormous trouble and expense to provide extra-curricular activities and sports with just this end in view. This represents an optimal degree of affirmation. The differences in this regard are strikingly brought out in the papers or project reports the students prepare. The eastern student, in his eagerness to persevere with the main theme leaves many secondary concepts without adequate definition. The western student endeavours, on the whole, to label and classify as many concepts as possible, thereby achieving maximal clarity.

Western societies with their emphasis on the tangible, consider individual man as the hub of the Universe. His movement in the existential dimension seems operate in the centrifugal pattern, from the centre to the periphery. Consequently, social systems in the West seem geared to man's maximal physical comfort and enjoyment. Again in the West, individual life is of extreme value and therefore the insistence on competition and individual enterprise. Capitalistic systems are seen to be the result. To an impartial observer belonging neither to the West nor to the East, it might seem that the concept of survival of the fittest, which seems to be implied in the operation of a capitalistic society has a connotation of intense selfishness. To offset this criticism, one must look at the great levelling influences built into the Western culture. Equality of individuals before the law, equality of educational opportunities for all, provision of some measure of advantage to handicapped people, guarantee of minimum wages and an adequate standard of living for all members of society, are some of the important measures put into operation to obviate the unfairness of a competitive society.

Eastern cultures seem to emphasise the reference of life, which has the implication that individual life is of secondary importance and that the welfare of the community comes first. This means that the Eastern movement is from the periphery towards the centre, in a centripetal direction. When the emphasis is on the community and not on the individual it would be apparent that socialistic processes would become evident in such cultures. This has largely been found to be true in the political life of the East. Perhaps it is a fallacy for political commentators to write ad nauseam that Eastern Societies succumb to socialistic patterns because of their poverty and that Western societies tend to be capitalistic because of their affluence. No evidence has come light to prove this contention. These writers have often fallen into the error rather common among researchers that if they find factors A& B together in a significant number of situations, either A has been responsible for B or B for A. Centripetal movements in the existential area especially amongst Eastern students in the Western World would perhaps explain why the former find it hard to understand the primary concern of the latter with competitiveness.

These cultural differences also carry over to concepts of religion, music and thinking. When individual man is considered the most important entity, it is easily understood as to why the West accepts vicarious experience as valid. For instance, the West accepts the possibility of one man dying for another and saving the second from damnation. The widespread acceptance of Christianity in the west with its doctrine of vicarious sacrifice is an instance in point. One man dying for another is far more heroic and important for the West rather than a man dying for some ideology or principle he has espoused. Specificity and limitation as to time and space are other outcomes of a centrifugal culture. Therefore human life has to be limited to a lifetime of meaningful experiences.

Centripetal civilisations would consider man to be the master of his destiny. Individual striving is emphasised because of the belief that no one can suffer for another nor expiate his sins. In other words man must accept full responsibility for his behaviour. The law of Karma, one of the cornerstones of Hindu philosophy and widely misunderstood in the West as a doctrine of fatalism, brings into focus the responsibility of man, how every action he performs must needs be accompanied by its consequences. The doer cannot absolve himself of responsibility for the consequence. He has to accept it as a law of nature. It is this acceptance that has been misunderstood as fatalism. The Law of Karma does not end there. It goes on to speak of the need for striving. Actions and their consequence follow one another but the doer is not passive. He should constantly strive towards his goal, sometimes despite overwhelming odds. Concepts of fatalism does not make sense in terms of centripetal ways of life, which must necessarily emphasise the responsibility of man for his actions.

An Easterner, especially a student, in the Western World in his struggle for successful coping with the environment can be seen to experience a conflict between his very human desire to rationalise failure as being due to exposure to an unfamiliar environment and his innate conviction that he himself is responsible for his lot.

Western concepts of living in closely-knit communities with a great deal of physical proximity of human beings at work and play result in communal togetherness. This may be seen to have the curious result of levelling individual differences amongst the members of a community and to lead to a greater strengthening of resources, which in turn could cater to the greater comforts of the individual. Eastern communities, despite their densities tolerate much more individuality amongst their members in that there is less of the stringent move towards cultural conformity. People from Eastern cultures can therefore be expected to find the Western scene somewhat of a paradox. The paradox is that while on the one hand Western societies encourage the tremendous drive towards competition, on the other they bring to bear a ruthless levelling influence, perhaps an attempt at restitution.

The thinking patterns of the east and West also seem to differ in a significant way. Individuals of a centripetal society seem to be divergent thinkers working from the concrete to the abstract. Their gestalt patterns of thinking often seem to lead to premature generalisations and syncretistic processes. Western thinking seems to be convergent, starting with a mass of data and working towards specific and limited conclusions. Consequent on this type of thinking is the avoidance of generalisations in a meticulous matter. Western thinking tends to emphasise objectivity while Eastern thinking relates more to the complementarity principle.

One of the crucial existential realities perceived differentially is the experience of suffering. In extraverted cultures, the members are encouraged to avoid suffering and as far as possible to savour only the pleasurable aspects of life. Most Western social systems seem geared to emphasise this very important habit pattern. Not only does this type of culture encourage individuals to eschew suffering, it also implies an aversion to perceive it in others. It would be expected therefore that centrifugal cultures would make use of repression to avoid all overt signs of grief or suffering. Eastern societies, while they do not especially enjoin their members to seek out suffering deliberately, try to teach men and women not to avoid pain or suffering when they do encounter it. A consequence of this is that members of a centripetal culture to experience suffering intensely and to be disinhibited in their overt expressions of grief.

In view of the characteristics referred to above, it would be a fair assumption that Western societies are goal oriented whereas the Eastern ones are process-oriented. In other words the former seem to emphasise consummatory behaviour whereas the latter consider the appetitive aspects as of being more important. Students of ethology would recognise appetitive behaviour as being preparatory in character and consummatory activity as being the end of preparatory behaviour. In Western technological societies propaganda through the mass media is directed towards getting its members to consume more and more goods. In the exploitation of natural resources also there does occur a desperate urgency. Building of taller and larger edifices within the shortest interval of time is another indication of consummatory behaviour. The system of going on holidays with its natural depletion of savings in one tremendous burst of enjoyment lasting for a few weeks, is yet another instance. One of the curious aspects of emphasis on consummatory activity is insistence on as painless a process as possible leading to the goal.

In considering Eastern Societies as being process-oriented, it is not meant that the goal is unimportant to them. The savouring of the process involved, in other words the full awareness of the nature of the path chosen to reach the ultimate goal is considered important and necessary. The belief in reincarnation demonstrates this emphasis very clearly. The concept of an individual striving through lifetime after lifetime and struggling hard to evolve himself into a perfect being, only to merge with the godhead demonstrates the great importance Eastern culture ascribed to appetitive behaviour.

Enough has been said above to emphasise the essential differences that could be said to exist between two extreme cultures. It may therefore be expected that any sallies from one culture by one of its members into the other, would create problems of adjustment and adaptation.

The difficulties referred to above are easily observed among young Asian students who go to Western countries to pursue a course of studies. Many of them, hailing from traditional societies are suddenly pitched into strange cultures, which expect not only an optimal level of initial functioning from the newcomer, but also a smooth transition into new behaviour patterns.

Although for the sake of clear definition, the introverted and extraverted cultures referred to above have been looked at in terms of Eastern and Western ones respectively, within each geographical group is a sub-group, which conforms to the other culture. Take Western society for instance. There is a minority in it, characterised by introversion and the conflict of this group with the majority throws up some very interesting existential aspects. The most apparent one concerns drug taking and the consumption of alcohol respectively. It is no accident then that most Western societies have accepted alcohol as a social beverage while legislating against the use of the so-called psychodelic drugs. Introverted cultures, on the other hand, have sought to introduce prohibitions against alcohol while tolerating if not entirely accepting the usage of such drugs as marijuana. Those who choose to study this matter closely would perhaps become aware of a pattern here. The consumption of alcohol in optimal quantities seems to disinhibit overt behaviour patterns and to enhance social bonhomie. By an extension of this idea, it might be seen that it also inhibits internal excitation, in other words the habit of looking within. In conformity with the concept of normality in the Western culture, alcohol can also been seen to facilitate aggressive behaviour, a modicum of which is tolerated or even encouraged in that culture. The use of marijuana in an extraverted culture would increase the introspective characteristics of the individual and enhance "internal excitation" very often inhibiting external behaviour. In introverted cultures, which consider an expansion of the internal experience as desirable and even pleasurable, these drugs in small quantities are seen as facilitating that aspect considered most important to human existence.

To sum it all up, it seems reasonable to assume that human cultures belong to either of two comprehensive groups, ones, which considers subjective experiences as having greater validity, and the other, which treats the objective phenomena as being of more importance. Various points of difference stemming from these approaches have been mentioned. The idea of this exercise has been to produce a hypothesis, which might function as a starting point for research into these matters.

From the point of view of the therapeutic system described in this book, clear delineation of aspects of introversion and extraversion are considered important. This is because the enlightened man, whatever his personal predilections, is supposed to desire greater awareness of himself and the external world. For the very extraverted person whose essays into the external world has been extensive, increased awareness means accentuated ability to look within. The introverted person on the other hand has had only limited encounters with the external world. Therefore, for him increased awareness would relate to the knowledge of the external environment. This system therefore proceeds from testable hypotheses and endeavours to develop that characteristic seen as deficient in the individual. That is why it has been referred to as a Gestalt approach as being applicable to all human beings, disturbed or considered "normal".

Sexual Behaviour

Until very recently, the culture of the Western World has largely been influenced by the fortunes of the church and the interpretation of its teachings. The early Roman and Greek Christians followed the sexual prohibitions of the orthodox Jews who considered marriage itself as a wholesome institution but denied the women of the time equality of status with men. (I sometimes wonder whether the status of women has changed all that much at present!). These Christians considered that the predominant function of marriage was for procreation. Celibacy and sexual abstinence were thought of as the highest Christian state; these concepts were largely initiated and shaped by St.Paul who himself remained a celibate all his life. Marriage itself was deemed to subserve some kind of compromise for people who fell short of the Christian ideal and it was thought, "it is better to marry than to burn". These modes of thought continued during the Patristic Age in which physical sexual relationships between married people continued to be regarded as a regrettable necessity. Disciplinary rules enjoined sexual abstinence during preparation for baptism and before receiving Holy Communion.

St. Augustine, who seemed to have had overwhelming sexual problems of his own, equated sexual indulgence with the fall of man and therefore as being intrinsically evil. However, marriage had the power to transform lust into a necessary duty, that of propagation of the human race. Even when these conditions were fulfilled, the transgression of the First Man would be transmitted to the child and hence the need for baptism. The dual standards of the time, while continuing to regard woman as the temptress and therefore denying to her any mercy were she caught in the act of adultery, permitted a great deal of sexual licence to the husband. Canons enacted during the first four centuries after Christ were against adultery, fornication, homosexuality, bestiality, abortion, desertion and bigamy.

During the Middle Ages, the important contribution to sexual thought was the idea developed by Peter Lombard and Thomas Aquinas that coition inherently good in itself, had been corrupted by the fall of man, which made for loss of control, the reference being to the inability of man to control ejaculation by the power of his will. Aquinas delineated a hierarchy of "crimes against nature" starting with masturbation up through unnatural positions and bestiality to the most serious of all–homosexuality. Man's authority over woman all through her life was emphasised by interpreting seduction and rape as the infringement of the rights of the girl's father and adultery as infringement of her husband's rights. Kissing and petting were permitted provided these could take place without any lustful indulgence. Prostitution, although evil in itself, was deemed to serve the useful function of preventing the more serious evil, homosexuality.

The main target of attack for the Reformers of the sixteenth century was clerical celibacy, which withheld from some the remedy (namely marriage) for temptation to unclean living. Both Calvin and Luther maintained the concept of the subordinate status of women although they permitted divorce and remarriage on a limited scale especially for men. The households of the Old Testament princes like Abraham, Isaac and Israel were held up as models with their patriarchal nature but without their polygamous aspects. Strangely enough, the Reformation brought in a modicum of prudishness in the Reformed Church as also in the Roman Catholic one. The four "causes" for marriage mentioned in the Book of Common Prayer, Procreation, remedy against sin, mutual society, help and comfort–perhaps sums up the conceptual attitude of the Reformed Church. Some semblance of sanctity was bestowed on the state of marriage by comparing it with the mystical union between Christ and the Church, this concept first seen in St. Paul's writings.

While there are many "enlightened" Christian opinions in the modern world, a large body of conservative thought remains male dominated and thus implicitly supports the dualistic standards always inherent in Christian thoughts on sex. The almost mystical concepts of the need to conserve semen and that its waste or misuse would result in punishment, physical and spiritual, although considered vestiges of medieval ideas, perhaps had and still have an adaptive function in ordering people's lives. However the propagation of these ideas have caused untold misery and guilt to a large number of young people in the West who do not know how to resolve the conflict between strong sexual urges and the necessity to avoid sin. Thus Christian thought on the subject of sex has been summed up as follows by a humanist:

For St. Paul, sex was wicked but enjoyable outside marriage and also wicked as well as enjoyable inside marriage.

For the Medieval Church, it was wicked but enjoyable outside marriage, and not wicked and not enjoyable inside marriage, but if enjoyed then wicked.

For the modern cleric however, it is wicked and not enjoyable outside marriage, not wicked and very enjoyable inside marriage.

The Church has a dilemma. Extensive studies such as the Kinsey Report and also the work of anthropologists, have disclosed the extent of ignorance regarding sexual matters among the general population. These have also confirmed a lurking suspicion that many of the so-called "perverted" sexual behaviour patterns are indeed widespread. The Christian Church today has an unenviable position as regards its attempts to interpret Biblical teachings in the light of socio-cultural developments in the modern world. Some of the questions it has been asked to answer include the following:

1. What is the Church's stand on premarital sexual relationships, promiscuous as also those between couples engaged to be married?

2. If it permits petting, caressing and such preparatory activities among unmarried people, how far can they go?

3. What are its teachings with regard to contraceptive practices within and without the marriage framework?

4. How should a Christian view trial marriages as a test of compatibility?

5. What of divorce?

6. Are there natural or divine laws regarding man's sexuality?

All these questions are of importance to Christians, non-Christians and even to atheists. Although it is easy to formulate questions, those which have been asked are significant in that they have been well thought out and couched in unambiguous terms shorn of mystical and perhaps moralistic connotations. These can be interpreted as a desperate cry for help from the young people of the world tortured by grave conflicts and whose very happiness and satisfactions depend on a resolution of sexual problems. To attempt to answer these questions seems a difficult task, if not an impossible one. Anyway it seems more economical to marshal facts and opinions for and against various patterns of sexual behaviour, taking into account the socio-psychological consequences these will have on the experiencing organism.

It is rather unfortunate that sexual attractions between men and women have been thought of as being synonymous with love. By doing this only a part of the gestalt is described. The Gestalt nature of love has been formulated in another chapter. It has been postulated that the love-gestalt is made up of a number of constituents some exerting more influence on the total behaviour than others. Looked at in this way, all love is essentially compounded of the same components which can be described as affection, tenderness, sexual expression and altruism, to quote just a few of the most important ones. Whereas the Freudian views emphasised the sexual determination of love, it would be more appropriate to consider sexuality as just one of the aspects of love. Whether it occupies a major role in the manifestation of love depends on the cultural, relational and environmental context in which it is expressed. There are many arguments for and against the consideration of the predisposition to love as an innate endowment. Nevertheless its relational expression and therefore the deterministic pattern of its components may be thought of as being shaped by the culture in which an individual happens to have his existence. One has only to consider, for example, the concept of incest. In the days of the early Egyptian Pharaohs, the marriage between brother and sister was an established institution and did not involve feelings of guilt because it was not considered incest. But this indulgence was available only to the Pharaohs and not to the common people of Egypt. Similarly in many cultures of the East and West cousin marriages are permitted, whereas in others they considered incestuous. Then there are a variety of mechanisms to ensure or avoid respectively endogamous or exogamous marriages, depending on the particular culture. This is not to say that there are not some forms of love relationships with similar patterns of expression, which have developed in the same way all over the world.

In the light of the consideration of love as a gestalt and sexual expression as just one aspect of it, we can perhaps interpret Freud's point of view on infant sexuality without recourse to the controversial connotations it has at present. The love of a boy towards his mother emphasises the components of tenderness, affection and longing, whereas that towards his father emphasises the expression of respect, regard and admiration. These differences in emphasis surely relate to the fact that the mother is a woman and that the father is a man. The former perhaps symbolises the child's tactile and oral satisfactions and the father's masculinity stands for disciplinary aspects and physical prowess, just to mention two. The thesis advanced here is that without necessarily invoking an Oedipal explanation for the relationship between a child and the parent of the opposite sex, the gestalt concept can perhaps explain the multifarious expressions of love as stemming from the same nature but differing in manifestation because this or that component has been predominantly emphasised in different human relationships. This differential emphasis could well be the product of cultural learning. By an extension of this idea it is easy to see how love relationships can turn awry (as in the case of incest) when due to faulty or inadequate learning, the appropriate emphasis has not been acquired by the particular individual.

Youth before marriage:

(a) Adolescence: Adolescence has been defined as a stage in life achieved by the process of acquiring the attitudes and beliefs needed for effective participation in society and as one of the periods of human development between the beginning of puberty and the attainment of adulthood. That adolescence need not necessarily be a time of storm and stress has been shown by anthropologists in their studies of Samoans among whom the adolescent is not required to inhibit overt sexual expression. As glandular changes and the development of secondary sexual characteristics are the essential features of this stage of life, the heterosexual desires which are awakened as a consequence have to find an outlet somehow. According to the Kinsey Report, masturbatory activity is widely practised among boys and girls, most of it surreptitiously, which generates varying amounts of guilt. Added to this is the widespread belief that the loss of semen would lead to anything from total exhaustion to mental illnesses. Both these are possible when there is massive guilt connected with the practice; this guilt can be seen as stemming from prohibitory parental and societal attitudes. Prohibition has been notoriously inefficient in causing a cessation of this habit. It is also not true to say there are no deleterious effects if guilt is avoided. For one thing, it is an activity in vacuo, which legitimately belongs to another context. For another, it is a decimation of the gestalt in that a whole segment of the stimulus complex, namely the presence of a loved member of the opposite sex, is missing. Thirdly, there is the attempt at restoration of the missing segment by indulging in fantasies, which might themselves become substitutions even when the experiencer gets married. In other words a fetish could be established, resulting in unsatisfactory sexual relationship with one's married partner. In extreme cases the habit of masturbation with wish-fulfilling fantasies may cause withdrawal reactions from an actual marriage. The current widespread view that this habit of self-stimulation has drive-reducing properties and therefore it helps to relax the youth is only partly acceptable to an existentialist. At the same time, it has to be recognised that the habit will be very difficult to eradicate from the life of the young. It is often found that societal or parental prohibition of any habit pattern (especially those which are pleasurable) does not lead to its elimination; it may even have the paradoxical effect of emphasising its attractiveness. The youth may cunningly device ways and means to hide his indulgence. A permissive matter of fact attitude towards this habit with attempts to provide a number of constructive activities to young people seems to be one way of affecting a compromise.

(b) Heterosexual behaviour:-

In Western societies, heterosexual courting behaviour starts rather early for a variety of reasons including cultural conditioning and the influence of the mass media, to quote just two. Very often the phenomenon that goes by the name of love seems to be sexual attraction, physical exploration and sensual arousal. This book being largely an exposition of the gestalt phenomenon, any description of sexual activity needs to be seen only as a delineation of how holistic or atomistic certain patterns of behaviour are. It is in that sense that the writer would like to say that most of the courting behaviour could truthfully be described as a sort of sexual hedonism. Despite all the satisfactions and pleasures that young people derive from such contacts, those who unwittingly choose the gestalt pattern, seem to be torn between their own strong sexual urges and the need to know how far they should go as regards physical contact. The resolution of such conflicts is not a simple matter unless the psychophysiological aspects of mating behaviour is analysed. In man this is of a very complex nature; it can be divided into two phases, the Appetitive Phase consisting of preliminary sexual activity and the Consummatory Activity, which is the actual act. Ethologists have demonstrated that in many infrahuman organisms appetitive behaviour is a true, purposive, adaptive and integrated activity capable of plastic response patterns; consummatory activity, on the other hand, is not under volitional control. This model fits human behaviour too. It is also possible that volitional control in human sexual behaviour is lost sometime before the actual sex act itself, which may be the reason why many well-meaning young couples in advanced stages of appetitive behaviour find themselves drawn into consummatory activity despite their conscious wishes not to do so. This sort of accident is very difficult to avoid so long as appetitive behaviour is heavily weighted in favour of physical exploration.

Western society has another problem in this context; having given cultural sanction to its young people to indulge in appetitive sexual behaviour, is it consonant with the physical and psychological health of these same youth to require them to stop short of consummatory activity? Physiologists have demonstrated that when stimuli cause arousal of glandular systems and mobilise the body for motor activity, if the consummatory activity does not take place, the tension state persists over a period of time. It is possible that habitual sexual arousal without consummatory satisfaction could cause emotional malaise.

Another significant development has been the progressive exposure to the male of greater unclothed areas of the female anatomy. It seems reasonable to assume that the threshold of sexual arousal in the male has become elevated because of adaptation to the constantly present stimuli. This, in turn, would mean that young people have to seek closer and more intimate physical contacts to enjoy erotic sensations even appetitive in character. Thus the range of appetitive behaviour seems to have become increasingly telescoped, with the possibility that the gap between it and consummatory behaviour has become narrowed.

This then is the dilemma. Society is prepared to let young men and women indulge in various levels of preparatory mating behaviour without letting them have the satisfaction of consummatory activity. In this campaign to contain sexual activity within bounds, fears of hell and judgment, of detection or infection and of pregnancy, have all been invoked in the past. None of these seem significant to the youth today. With all these fears removed, there seems no reason whatever to prevent young people going the whole way. At present it is a widespread practice to provide contraceptive knowledge and advice to children so that the risk of illegitimate pregnancy can be avoided. Many people who do not object to limited sexual exploration in young people still do not take into account the psychological consequences of a young couple knowing each other. Alex Comfort, a knowledgeable man in the field says: "For the girl, every act of penetration, then or later, is an invasion of her body by forces outside herself. She can never feel exactly the same towards a man who has 'known' her thus, even if only once."

J.D. Unwin sums up the body of evidence in favour of pre-marital chastity in these words: "Any society in which pre-nuptial sexual freedom has been permitted for at least three generations will be in the Zoistic condition. The Zoistic condition represents the most primitive and least inherently civilised form of religious and social patterns and having the lowest capacity for development into a higher pattern. Dr. David Mace thinks that "this gives scientific validity to a fact which always been tacitly recognised, that the relaxation of sexual restraint has invariably led to the downfall of civilisation."

Marriage and Morals:-

Studies of sexual behaviour seem to suggest that a fair proportion of young brides are already pregnant at the time of their marriage. Clear statistics are not available as to what percentage of these brides had to rush into an unscheduled marriage because of their pregnancy and how many got that way because of sexual activities with their fiancés. This writer does not propose to examine the question as to whether or not marriage should be considered a sacrament. Nor does he wish to consider the moral aspects because it seems reasonable to assume that the adaptiveness of a piece of behaviour is the chief criterion for most therapists. Adaptiveness of behaviour itself is seen as contributory to the greater actualisation of a human being's potential and not as a mere coping mechanism. Even the most enthusiastic advocate of sexual freedom would admit that the relationship between lovers has something that transcends mere sensuality. Again it is an emphasis on the gestalt aspect of love, the concept that the whole is more than the sum of its parts. As with all gestalt concepts, the attribute, which makes for this phenomenon is hard to qualify and difficult still to quantify. This does not mean that some mystical and intangible entity has been added on to the sum of the parts but that only the inter-relationship among the constituents creates the gestalt. In the intimate relationship between a man and a woman this something could perhaps be seen as the avoidance of pre-marital sexual indulgence. Again this has no moralistic connotation. Many men and women have been able to have premarital sexual relationships without feeling guilty about it and without experiencing any decimation of their gestalt love. These fortunate people are very few in number. The average but reasonably sophisticated person is context bound in the sense that what is appropriate in one situation is not so in another. In fact this field-orientation is what is termed gracious living. Such a man is not merely content with creature comforts; he relentlessly seeks to surround himself with beautiful things and aesthetic situations. There is no need to consider only marriage as an exception to the general search for the beautiful.

Compatibility:-

One of the major aspects of marriage is compatibility which can be defined as the ability of a couple to adjust to each other through all manner of experiences, pleasant as also unpleasant. Psychologists and counsellors now agree that any human being within society has to be able to communicate. But the level, quality and quantity of communication can differ between the same two people on different occasions and different situations. The problem of communication between married couples relates to the ratio of verbal versus nonverbal communication. In many societies verbal communication has greater acceptability than the non-verbal. Perhaps it is possible to look at a model in which the total volume of communication between a married couple is considered to be a constant with the proviso that this "reservoir" can differ from couple to couple but with the same couple it should remain the same all through the vicissitudes of life. If such a model is at least considered a working hypothesis, it is possible to see the interaction between a husband and wife, in terms of verbal and non-verbal communication patterns. Although it might seem that when the ratio between these two forms of communication favours the verbal it is considered an adaptive interaction, a predominance of nonverbal communication has sometimes been a sign or consequence of marital harmony. On the other hand, a predominance of verbal communication could sometimes evince itself as arguments and quarrels. Although individual couples might differ in the "baseline' communication pattern, marital harmony or lack of it at any point in time can be seen as the lack of deviation or the amount of deviation respectively from the "basic ratio". It is now possible to look at the concept of compatibility. When married couples tend to take each other for granted, verbal communication perhaps becomes sparse and warped. Theoretically the answer to this lies, in the setting right of the communication ratio, which has gone awry, rather than in the dissolution of such a marriage.

The question of compatibility arises long before marriage, as soon as a man and woman even think of setting up a meaningful relationship. Some people advocate long engagements giving the intending couple an opportunity to be sure of their mutual compatibility before embarking on a life together. But such "rational' pre-nuptial judgments of compatibility take into account only the individual characteristics of each person and not the adjustment which is a progressive interactional process; more often than not adjustment processes occur at a subliminal level. Secondly, the sense of belongingness and possession, which people develop after marriage, changes their attitude towards each other. Trial marriages have been advocated as a test of compatibility before a couple sets up home together. Many of the arguments advanced above seem to militate against the institution of trial marriages, plus the fact that under those circumstances sexual expression would perhaps be too greatly emphasised at the expense of the other components of the love-gestalt. It is also common knowledge that sexual adjustment together with all other aspects of love, grow on a married couple and that it takes years before their interaction is shorn of its rough edges. In a large percentage of marriages continuous and continued interaction in all aspects of personality is necessary before adjustment, even of a workable nature, is accomplished. Trial marriages can perhaps be seen as mere rationalisations to support unlimited and in some ways not very responsible sexual behaviour.

Freedom in Marriage:-

The Biblical concept that after marriage a couple becomes "one flesh" in terms of the interactional analysis referred to above, can be taken to mean not only the intimate nature of the physical relationship which does accomplish this in a sexual sense, but it also can refer to the deeper psychological awareness of each one's identity in relation to the other. To talk of the need for freedom of action by either of the parties carries perhaps the connotation that the husband or the wife should be able to act without reference to the other. This is like advocating the right of an individual in a democratic society to behave without much consideration of others simply because the individual according to law, has freedom of action. Freedom presupposes action within a frame of reference and therefore carries with it the connotation of limitation. Thus any freedom becomes chaotic if individuals acted independently of one another. Much criticism has been levelled at the promise "to love and obey" in the marriage service. This seems to many people the perpetuation of male supremacy alien to this era of emancipated women. Consonant with the evolution of the present-day social system, it does not seem an anachronism if this behest were to be interpreted to mean "to do something at the request of, or to please the marriage partner." It is perhaps a sign of lack of consistency in thinking, that obedience to the law of the land is considered wholesome whereas obedience of a couple to each other in marriage is considered an absence of freedom.

According to Alex Comfort "It has been said that men as opposed to women are poly-erotic but monogamous." He goes on to say that very many men and women are sincerely capable of loving two people at once without making unfavourable comparisons between them. The initial development of the concept of love as a gestalt in this book does not preclude the idea of such relationships.

The unfavourable comparisons that an erring husband or wife does not make, stem from the possibility that the love gestalt in each of these relationships can have a differential emphasis. Marriage counsellors are aware that many a poly-erotic husband often withholds from his own wife spontaneous sexual contacts while lavishing "affection" on her in many other ways.

One of the strange phenomena demonstrating the interdependence between marriage partners is the see-saw effect in which the husband and wife each reciprocally alternates between a sense of wellbeing and psychopathology. While this system is grossly seen in disturbed families, there is no reason to suppose that in normal marriage relationships this kind of homeostatic device is absent. It is as if the total energy in the system is constant and when there is more intensity of wellbeing in one of the partners the other must proportionately feel out-of-sorts.

Divorce:

People who oppose the doctrine that a married couple lives together till death do part them, say that it is immoral to force two unwilling people to live together even when they have outlived their love for each other. In 1966 a committee of clergy and laity presented a report to the British Council of Churches, which supported a case for divorce in some marriages. Where one of the partners has some condition of physical or mental illness which makes it difficult to hold the marriage together or that in which the incompatibility at the personality level is so great as to cause constant and persistent mutual irritation, a dissolution of the marriage seems unavoidable. To make divorce easy to obtain thereby letting people go about changing marital partners, would perhaps be distasteful to progressive thinkers mainly because of the psychological implication that the hallmark of an adjusted personality is a modicum of consistency in behaviour patterns. This is apart from ethical and aesthetic values that particularly Christians of the West seem to emphasise. It is true that changes of marital partners do provide a variety of sexual pleasures but not happiness or security, as many of the much-married films starts of America have confessed time and again. Moreover this kind of behaviour seems to be one-sided, as mainly men seem to profit from it. This is not due to any fall from virtue these essays constitute, but only because it is perhaps a universal human experience that happiness cannot be brought about by direct intent but seems to exist as a by-product and that security is a consequence of enduring frames of reference. Despite all these considerations, were human societies to abandon restraints that hold people together in marriage, there could well be chaos. It is an empirical observation that in a healthy human being various aspects of physiological, psychological and intellectual mechanisms do not continue to grow indefinitely but achieve maturation towards the end of adolescence. Social scientists have demonstrated how difficult it is to change attitudes and frames of reference. Hence the drastic techniques, revolting to the freedom loving man, used in brain washing which are aimed at such changes. In the pursuit of sensual pleasure, were man called upon to change his frames of reference constantly as would be necessary if he had to adjust to every new marital partner, his psychological homeostatic processes could well go awry with consequent neurotic breakdowns. It seems clear therefore that while licence as regards sexual promiscuity may perhaps be ruled out for reasons predominantly of a psychological nature, sometimes divorces may have be sanctioned also out of sheer necessity to preserve the integrity of personality. A satisfactory compromise has yet to be worked out.

Children:

Even the most militant advocates of sexual freedom and those who propound doctrines of zero population growth, would perhaps accept that children have to be born although their number needs to be restricted in a planned manner. To make Planned Parenthood possible, there should be men and women, especially the latter, willing to achieve that status. It does not require a great stretch of imagination to visualise the fact that responsible parenthood and sexual promiscuity have a reciprocal relationship. This means that at least some percentage of married couples should stick together "for better or worse, for richer or poorer, in sickness and in health" for the sake of preventing extinction of the human species. Another possibility is that even men and women who desire change of marital partners can, or may desire to have children who would then be placed under the custodial care of the State. The State, in turn, can establish institutions for these children thereby letting the parents free to resume their own individual lives, together or with other partners. However, it remains clear that women having the responsibility of conceiving children stand to have somewhat restricted freedom than men.

Margaret Ribble, Rene Spitz, Bowlby and other careful investigators have demonstrated that children deprived of satisfactory supervision by loving adults do develop emotional maladies some which have been referred to as 'negativism' 'anaclitic depression, and 'hospitalism' to quote just a few. They have also demonstrated permanent scars to the personality by continued deprivation of this kind. Some studies of the children in foundling homes, which had surrogate mothers available, have also demonstrated similar effects due to inadequate mothering. The conclusion seems to be that there is rarely a substitute for the real mother and therefore it might be a psychological and social necessity for parents of the children to remain as a unit. The proponents of family therapy have brought out the importance of the father as an essential element in the family dynamics. They further emphasise the concepts of intrafamilial equilibrium and processes of homeostasis. There is another reason why family units have to be preserved. Unless by some miraculous genetic determination the drive towards motherhood that most women seem to want can be abolished or modified, the need for parenthood would continue. In some women whose mothering behaviour gets disturbed due to accidental hormonal imbalance the sexual urge also has been seen to have disappeared or to have diminished. It seems clear then that there exist far-reaching consequences to promiscuous sexual behaviour, when these are considered against the advantage of stable and lasting marriages, the latter seems to outweigh the former.

The Law:-

It is not the aim of the writer to discuss the existence and application of a universal moral law, the obedience to which results in the greater happiness of man. The natural laws of sexual behaviour have already been interpreted in terms of psycho-socio-biological contrasts. In most Western societies, there are distinct mores about deviant sexual practices and laws have been promulgated regarding these. Some of these laws seem to be harsh in that they are retributory in nature, having very little deterrent value. The modification of behaviour patterns and provision of socialisation do not seem to have been taken into account. Some of the witch-hunts that go on under the guise of self-righteousness could well be a kind of reaction formation. It has to be granted that many of the sexual aberrations are inconvenient and embarrassing to society; therefore certain restrictive measures become necessary. But these should be aimed at allowing the erstwhile deviant to rehearse modified and socially acceptable sexual behaviour patterns by sampling progressive approximations to the real environment; in other words he is given the benefit of a graded pattern of learning. Time was, not so long ago that homosexuality was singled out for the greatest social condemnation although it causes perhaps the least harm to the parties concerned. Other types of sexual deviation including promiscuity need to be considered as psychological disturbances of varying degrees of severity. Learning theorists have demonstrated that punishment of a socially undesirable response leads to less therapeutic success than the rewarding of socially acceptable responses. In terms of the gestalt theme set out in this book, therapeutic measures to deal with all manner of sexual deviations would be interpreted as attempts to wean away the deviant by changing the emphasis of his love-gestalt through the rewarding of hitherto unreinforced but socially acceptable components of it.

A Summing Up:-

In summing up, we can say that there is a number of progressive points of view, some radical, some others extremely conservative and yet others occupying various intermediate points in regard to sexual behaviour in men and women. In this chapter, an attempt has been made to present a Gestalt view consonant with the psycho-socio-biological consequences of man's behaviour in this field. It has further been emphasised that the existing bewilderment and promiscuity in sexual behaviour are, in a large measure, due to dissociation of the sensual aspect of sex from the love gestalt of which it forms part. Two aspects of total sexual behaviour were considered, the appetitive phase which is goal oriented as also adaptive, and the consummatory activity which is not under voluntary control. Due to the conditions of modern living, the threshold of sexual arousal has become progressively elevated resulting in young people having to seek more and more intimate physical contact for arousal. Promiscuous sexual intercourse has become safer on account of the eradication of the four basic fears, hellfire, detection, disease and conception. But the psychological consequences of a man and a woman "knowing" each other in a sexual sense are deep and intensely meaningful. There are certain responsibilities connected with sexual behaviour when children are born within and out of marriage. Institutional care of children is possible so that men and women are freed to resume some amount of hedonistic pursuits including sexual activity. Researchers have demonstrated that children deprived of adequate mothering are prone to develop serious emotional difficulties. Irresponsibility and sexual hedonism by parents would thus entail the possibility of mental illness for their children brought up in impersonal institutional environments. Hence enduring monogamous marriages seem to be a necessary compromise. Divorces seem justifiable only under exceptional circumstances and should be supervised in a better fashion than has been possible so far. The family itself is now being considered a dynamic unit with levels of equilibrium brought about by predictable homeostatic processes.

The attitude of the community towards sexually deviant behaviour still remains unenlightened due to the failure to make a clear-cut distinction between the doer and the deed. A gestalt approach (to which cognitive behaviour therapy techniques seem to be the nearest approximation) tends to avoid value judgments on the doer while evaluating the social adaptiveness of the deed. Acceptance of the Gestalt approach would necessitate rethinking about the punitive aspects of law enforcement prevalent in today's society. Laws regarding sexual deviations seem discriminatory and are in dire need of revision. In the ultimate analysis it has to be emphasised that individual man's pursuit of sexual pleasures can yield satisfactions only in so far as his liberty to do so does not clash with the liberties of others to act in a similar manner.

Concepts Of Death

The average adult seems embarrassed if anyone he is with brings up the topic of death. To him it is a morbid subject, which like religion, should be eschewed at all costs. Some others in this culture rationalise their avoidance of the subject by comparing death with the atmosphere around us. The air with its life-sustaining oxygen is with us always; no one speaks about it because it is an essential part of our lives. So it is with death, they claim. All human beings must die. As death is inevitable, it does no one any good to talk about it. Yet, the development of attitudes towards death is not accidental; nor is it entirely shaped by cultural factors.

To examine concepts of death it is useful to investigate ontogenetic developmental aspects. In a systematic study by Maria N. Nagy, children between the ages of 7 and 10 were asked to write compositions in response to the general instruction "Write down everything that comes to your mind about death." The children were also asked to make drawings of themes that occurred to them in connection with the subject. Following this the experimenters held discussions with every child regarding his/her writing and drawing. Some children between the ages of 3 and 6 sampled in this study were merely interviewed and encouraged to talk about their ideas and feelings about death. Altogether about 378 children living and around Budapest participated in this study.

The results of this investigation dispelled the notion that very young children have neither a meaningful idea on death nor have they thought about it in a significant way. It was found that children below the age of 5 years thought of death as a parting or as sleep. Many children in this age group perceived death as a temporary parting, the dead person continuing his existence elsewhere under changed circumstances. It is also significant that they imagined inanimate objects and dead people alike as living in a separate world. This then is the stage of animism.

The second stage in the development of attitude occurs between the ages of 5 and 9. Children of this age tend to personify death and talk of it as a person. It was also seen that they very often interchanged the words death and the dead. This stage has been referred to as anthropocentric because the child of this age believes that every change, even in the outside world is brought about by man.

Children above the age of 9 seem to consider death as a process as do most adults. At this stage again the child's concepts of the world and experiential patterns are reflected in his attitude towards death. Every child has two basic items of curiosity, about sex and about death expressed by two implicit questions, Whence came I and Whither go I? Even when a young person has acquired the concept of death as a process, which happens to every human being, it remains largely an intellectual idea isolated from appropriate emotions. This is mostly because of the avoidance reaction that prevents a person from discussing this topic with others. Most Western cultures bring up their children with an implicit taboo concerning death as a topic of conversation. Consequently an adult who can be considered mature in very many ways tends to think of death as something that happens to other people; but he himself seems to be safe from this universal predator. The only way of interpreting this conception of personal immortality seems to invoke a kind of denial.

Some amount of pessimism can be seen in the Freudian concept which postulates two main instincts in human beings, the Eros or the Life instinct and the Thanatos, the Death instinct respectively. These two opposing drives are seen to exist simultaneously in all human beings. Presumably it is the balance between these two, which determines whether a person is going to be cheerful and highly motivated or depressed and disinterested. Whatever the state of equilibrium of Eros and Thanatos, the latter denotes a progression towards inanimation and the attainment of inorganicity. Nirvana, which Freud postulated as the end product of the drive, that Thanatos initiates, is not the bliss of Hindu philosophy but of nothingness. In the early development of the male child, the Oedipus Complex, which stems from the ambivalent attitude of the child towards its father and its desire to possess the mother, evokes the first great fear in the child that the father might wreak vengeance on him for daring to be his rival. A man-child interprets the impending punishment as one that would deprive him of his genital organs. Interpreting Freud' writings, it would appear that this fear perhaps motivates the infant boy to take more interest in the father and to try to identify with him. By such a subtle strategy the boy succeeds in putting away his fear of castration; Freud refers to this process as Repression. Repressed ideas are not erased but only kept away from awareness by anti-cathectic forces. Repressed ideas have also the incorrigible habit of trying to intrude under various guises into consciousness. In adult life when people have the fear of death, it is seen under Freudian psychology as a reactivation of the infantile castration fear.

Most Christian denominations inculcate in their followers the idea of eternal life and of this earth as being a testing ground for one's suitability to enter into everlasting bliss. The alternative, believed in by some Christians, is complete destruction or eternal torment. Implicit in the belief in eternal life is the concept of Death as a gateway or as a threshold to more meaningful experiences. It might be worthwhile to consider how peoples of many religions look at the aftermath of death.

Christians believe in a soul, which leaves the body after death. Here again there are differences in views depending on the denomination to which they belong. Protestants believe that the souls after separation from the body wait for the final judgment when God separates the sheep from the goats. When this happens, the souls are rejoined with the bodies that they inhabited while on earth. This is the first resurrection. At the final judgment those who are not adjudged good enough to go to heaven are consigned to everlasting hell. The righteous souls then go to Heaven to live with God for all eternity. However, there are some who do not believe there is a Hell. They believe that God the All merciful and Kind, will not consign human beings to everlasting torment on the basis of the actions that they carried out in the space of a single lifetime. All this becomes particularly relevant when we go through the Bible carefully. In the First Chapter of Genesis (the first book of the Bible) we read: "And God said, Let us make man in our image, after our likeness: and let them have dominion over the fish of the sea and over the fowl of the air, and over the cattle and over all the earth, and over every creeping thing that creepeth over the earth." Many Christians have never perhaps thought deeply about what it all means. When the Bible says that God made man in His image, it does not mean that man is an exact copy of God. In fact man became a little like God after Adam and Eve had eaten of the tree of Knowledge of Good and Evil. But the important difference that still exists is that man can die but God cannot. Especially after the disobedience of Adam and Eve, lest they eat of the fruit of the tree of Life, God drove them out of the Garden of Eden and put an Angel with a flaming sword to prevent man from having access to eternal life.

What of the soul of man? The Hebrew word for Soul, Nephesh, means living being. In the second chapter of Genesis we read: "And the Lord God formed man of the dust of the ground and breathed into his nostrils the breath of life, and man became a living soul" By the same token, everything that has life, is a living soul. Perhaps it would be relevant here to refer to the Hindu concept of Prana (breath), which also means the same thing. The question then arises, can the soul die? In the book of Ezekiel it says, "The soul that sinneth, it shall die." A careful perusal of the Bible discloses that it speaks of two deaths for living beings. After the first death there is absolute unconsciousness until the souls of the just and the unjust are resurrected within the bodies they had had in the first instance. This means that when they are resurrected, they will have the same mind and characteristics they had when they were alive on earth. All souls are then judged according to their actions. Those who are deemed to have striven after righteousness go into everlasting life and those who have been gross sinners suffer their second death from which there is no awakening. This means that the wicked, instead of being thrown into everlasting unquenchable fire in Hell, suffer absolute destruction.

The word hell means to cover or to hide. The Hebrew word **Sheol** has been used for Hell in the translation of the King James version of the Bible. A place in the Bible where Sheol is defined is found in Ecclesiastes in chapter 9 where it says "For the living know that they shall die: but the dead know not anything, neither have they any more a reward; for the memory of them is forgotten. Also their love, and their hatred, and their envy, is now perished; neither have they any more a portion for ever in anything that is done under the sun…Whatsoever thy hand findeth to do, do it with all thy might; for there is no work, nor device, nor knowledge, nor wisdom in the grave (sheol) where thou goest." Thus the concept of unconsciousness after death has been emphasised.

Some mention has to be made of Lucifer commonly known as Satan. He was one of the brightest and noblest of the Archangels of God. He was not always wicked. The name Lucifer itself means **Light Bearer**. We read in Isaiah "How art thou fallen from heaven, O Lucifer, son of the morning! How art thou cut down to the ground, which didst weaken the nations?" His problem was not basically wickedness of the kind we know in human relations but his rebellion against the authority of God. For some reason he began to think that God was being unfair to him, which of course was not true. In the Garden of Eden in his encounter with Eve, when she mentioned that God had said the moment she partook of the fruit of the Knowledge of Good and Evil she would die, Lucifer asserted that she would surely not die. Like many other things in the Bible one could ask why God allowed Satan to live in the Garden of Eden and why did He allow this encounter with Eve when He knew what the outcome would be. Perhaps the persuasion of Eve to disobey God was the first success Lucifer had in his grand plan. From then on, he set out to seduce human beings. We read in the Book of Job that he entreated God to let him try to wean Job off his dependence on the Goodness of God. It is written that God agreed. But then unlike Eve, Job was not a soft touch and Satan failed to persuade Job to "curse God and die." It might be a good place here to introduce to the reader the book **Sorrows of Satan** by Marie Corelli in which she brings out the essential goodness of Satan and how when a human being rejects his advances, he is allowed to reach the portals of Heaven to hear the Angels sing! In short, despite the depredations of Satan in human affairs, he still remains a gentlemanly and noble being who has to be pitied rather than hated.

Fanatical Christians, who perhaps misread the Bible, think that God takes pleasure in watching the wicked burn continually in the unquenchable fire of Hell. In Ezekiel we read: "As I live, saith the Lord, I have no pleasure in the death of the wicked, but that the wicked turn from his way and live." When wickedness gets out of hand, it is true that retribution overtakes the wicked, as happened to the people of Sodom and Gomorrah who were destroyed completely. It is said that God rained brimstone and fire to destroy the people of those cities.

Many theologians of the Catholic Church believe that for sinners who had not had the opportunity to repent their sins committed during their lives on earth do get a second chance to do penance in a place referred to as Purgatory. The "burning away of their sins" in Purgatory can also cause intolerable pain, as St. Augustine makes clear in his writings. But then the suffering of the sinners in Purgatory can expiate their sins making them ready to enter into everlasting life with God. Thus Catholics believe that people do get a second chance after death to get themselves purified from sin. An outcome of this belief is that living people can pray for the dead so that they may be helped to expiate their sins. Further, the protestant belief that after death there is total unconsciousness for the soul until the resurrection does not have validity for the Catholics. The question has also been asked as to whether the souls in purgatory can pray for us who are living in the world. Catholic Theologians seem to think that they can pray for the living and their intercession with God will be helpful. All this seems a bit complicated, but the point is that human beings do get a second chance to get rid of their sins.

Hinduism believes in an immortal soul, which is indestructible. The Bhagavad-Gita clearly says: "The Soul who dwells within the body can never be slain". More than that, the Atman (the individual soul) is an exact copy of the Paramatman (God). (This is at variance with the Christian belief that God and man are not exactly the same in characteristics). Thus the Hindu belief is that the soul of man is divine and that this divinity pervades the whole of the Universe. The body is but a temporary vehicle for the Soul to operate from. Only the body dies but not the Soul. Salvation for the Hindu is actually Self-realisation, that the atman is divine. Once that realisation is achieved, there is nothing more for the Soul to do. What is more, the interminable chain of births and rebirths consequent on Karmic involvements is broken once and for all. Most Hindus believe that once this is achieved, the Atman merges with the Paramatman. This is equivalent to Heaven and is termed Moksha. There are four paths laid down in Hindu scriptures for the attainment of Self-Realization namely Bhakthi Yoga, Karma Yoga, Gnana Yoga and Raja Yoga respectively. The Hindus and the Buddhists believe in the multi-life theory as against the Christian concept of only one life on this earth.

Although Buddha accepted the basic Hindu doctrines of karma and reincarnation, he asserted that desire is what keeps us bound to the cycle of death and rebirth. The Buddhist concept of Nirvana means the extinction of desire when one becomes liberated. They have also the doctrine of "anatta" which means that individuals do not possess eternal souls but a bundle of habits, memories, sensations, and desires, which results in the delusion that they have a lasting self. Despite its transitory nature the false self exists as a unit even reincarnating in body after body. When the idea of the false self is abandoned there is nothing to reincarnate and nothing to experience pain. According to Tibetan Buddhism, the spirit of the dead goes through a process lasting 49 days divided into three stages known as "bardos." After this the person either enters Nirvana or has a rebirth. Moreover, the last thoughts that a dying individual has, influences the nature of one's reincarnation. Up to four days after death may be the time required for the departed to realise that the body has been dropped. Everyone gets a fleeting experience of a clear light at the moment of death. The more spiritually developed you are the longer you have the consciousness of light. In the stage two the departed can have hallucinations depending on his karmic experiences. Very highly evolved individuals can enter directly into a paradise realm.

The Muslims also believe in a spirit living within the body and which is moulded constantly according to the deeds of the person concerned. If good deeds are done, the spirit is nourished, but if evil deeds are performed these leave their mark on the spirit. After death the spirit lives on. The Heaven and Hell that are spoken about, come about in this world. The warm glow that we feel inside when we do good is a harbinger of the Heaven to come. The guilt and sorrow consequent on the performance of evil deeds represent Hell in this world. There are no words to convey to us the concepts of Heaven and Hell after the spirit leaves the body. Therefore we speak of pleasant gardens and rivers in Heaven. We also speak of torments and fire in Hell. Actually the experience of Heaven and Hell starts in this world itself. The Muslims believe in the Day of Judgment when the spiritual world is brought into full manifestation. It is then that the fruits of one's actions on this earth are fully experienced. Those who have the fortune to have the pleasant experience of Paradise will have the chance to evolve still further. Those who are suffering the effects of their evil deeds are not "punished" eternally but they also have a chance to make amends and to grow into righteousness. This means there is no everlasting punishment for anyone. Muslims do not believe in reincarnation. Once the spirit leaves the body at death there is no coming back to this world in further births.

It is clear then that in most religions of the world there is the belief in an entity that survives bodily death. This entity is often referred to as the soul. While most Christian denominations believe that there is only one existence for the body on this earth, the Hindus believe that the soul can reincarnate in a new body. They believe it is possible to have thousands or even millions of reincarnations till the soul has achieved enlightenment.

Most people believe that the phenomenon of death is something to be feared. They think that there is tremendous amount of suffering involved at the moment life leaves the body. But the accounts of near-death-experiences by people who have almost died but were brought back to life by suitable resuscitation methods do not bear this out. It is common for people at the point of death to speak of a tunnel through which they pass. At the end of the tunnel is a shaft of soft light and there are beings in shining clothes who welcome the "soul" into their new domain. A cardiac patient who was on the point of death had this to say. He was floating up and up until he came to a huge face of Jesus Christ at the end of this tunnel. The face was very kindly and it said to him: "Your time has not yet come. You have to go back." The next thing he knew, the doctors were thumping on his chest. Some other patients speak of clearing the end of the tunnel but the shining beings at the other side telling them to go back. It is clear that the belief of the dying person about what lies beyond has a great deal to do with the experience of death. For those who believe in a wonderful place to go to will have peace, happiness and joyful expectation; for them death is not to be feared at all.

Perhaps existential viewpoints of death are varied but they all seem to convey some aspects of meaning to the existence provided by the prospect of death. Viktor Frankl seen as an existentialist thinks that the finiteness of human life endows existence with significance. If we were immortal we could with impunity postpone every action forever. But the certainty of death ushers in a kind of urgency to life. This means that all human beings have to utlise their lifetimes to the utmost. Frankl, when emphasising the individual's responsibility towards his own existence, brings out the interesting idea that a person should act "as if" he were carrying out every action for the second time and that the act in question was wrongly executed on the first occasion. This again emphasises the urgency of life in which one cannot afford to make mistakes. Even when adequate deliberation and care have been exercised it is possible that one could be "called away" before one's task has been completed. Frankl considers unfinished work also as fulfillment. While existentialists have often considered the significance of suicide in terms of fulfillment, Frankl's concept only tends to signify the ability of a human being within the framework of his will to do with life as he chooses, or to end it after responsible decision. Studying Frankl's works, it becomes immediately apparent that his Christian approach is characterized by hope and optimism the human being usually can choose to bring meaning to life. Not so with all existentialists although they would all hold that life has meaning in connection with death. Heidegger clarifies the seemingly obvious concept that death is one thing no one else can do for "me." Its terror or pain or anguish has to be experience by me, all in the fullness of time. Quoting the poignant work of Tolstoy "The death of Ivan Ilych" he goes on to say that most people in Western cultures tend to detach themselves so much when talking or thinking of death that when talking or thinking of death that they say to themselves "One dies" instead of "I shall die". This verbalisation has the function of insulating the individual against a head-on encounter with the idea of death. Consciousness of death shatters the banality of everyday existence and liberates us from the petty mentality of the ordinary man. Heidegger thinks that this consciousness heightens self-awareness and confers upon us the state of individuality. The terror of death that is maintained by our holding on to the flimsy concept of personal immortality can be overcome by actively assuming a Being-for-Death (Sein-Zum-Tode) attitude.

Sartre makes a distinction between the ultimate subjective possibility and the function of death. A person's death could be conceptualised in either way. If for instance death is considered as something that happens to me, then no one else can die for me. If on the other hand, I have to die for a cause, then the functional aspect is emphasised; in that case anyone else can die in my place for the cause espoused. Heidegger's formulation about the individuality conferred by death on a person, can also be looked at under the dichotomous categories mentioned above. To do this clearly we need to study the broad types of the death experience that one comes across. First of all there is death by suicide. If suicide is only a means to an end, in other words the means of serving a cause, then the meaning conferred by death is not on life but on the cause, which has been championed. The recent proliferation of suicide bombers poses a very complex situation that cannot be looked at here at the present time. It confers individuality and meaning to life only if we are projecting ourselves towards death as an ultimate possibility.

Sometimes death occurs at an appointed time. This is seen when a condemned man is executed or when a man dies of a fatal disease. The experiencer does not fix the time or manner of death but these are fixed for him by an outside authority thus robbing him in one fell swoop of futurity and the possibility of projection of himself towards a meaningful existence. Summing up Sartre's conceptualisation, his philosophy can be simplified in this manner: "Death is never that which gives life its meaning; it is on the contrary that which on principle removes all meaning from life." However, both Heidegger and Sartre grant that man in usual circumstances has freedom to be and that death has some unmistakable significance for the individual himself.

For some strange reason existentialists have not quoted the instance of Sydney Carton in the Tale of Two Cities or of the robber crucified with Jesus and who sympathised with the latter's plight. Sydney Carton was a drunkard whose life seemed to lack purpose; or so it seemed to the people around him. But the death which he voluntarily chose namely to die in his friend's stead bestowed on his nondescript life a meaning not only in the eyes of the world but also in his own. It seemed to have raised his self-esteem and to have pulled him out of his habitual pattern of self-devaluation. In the case of the robber who was crucified with Jesus, death could not bestow meaning to a life misspent but it did restore his peace of mind and his feeling of himself as a person.

In the main there seem to be two views of life prevalent in human societies. Those that emphasise competitiveness and capitalism tend also to emphasise the value of individual life. They tend to encrust the individual with social welfare facilities and to try to prolong his life as much as possible. Even people in the terminal stages of a fatal illness tend to be protected from death and to be encouraged to eke out their pitiful existence to the last gasp. In such societies, it stands to reason that people should be afraid of death and to avoid talking about this. The second concept is the reverence for life, which carries more of a collective connotation. All life is valuable and therefore to be revered. Societies that emphasise reverence for life rather than its value seem to take the position of Being-for-Death conceptualised by Heidegger. It would be expected that the absence of implicit taboo regarding death as a discussion topic would enable members of such a society to be able to come to grips with the idea of themselves having to die one day.

Again societies that emphasise nuclear family structures seem to provide separate homes for the Senior Citizens where the aged relatives eke out their last days in an institutionalised atmosphere. It is not just an accident that young people seem to reject the old; it may be that the latter remind the former of the days when they themselves would have progressed on the path of certain dissolution. When there is a taboo on speech about a certain topic, it is but a logical step to go on to the not-thinking response that in turn leads to the shutting out from awareness of the idea itself.

The persistent worldwide agitation against war in Afghanistan and Iraq has been labelled as the youthful protest against conformity and double-dealing. Altruism and idealistic predilections have been evoked as legitimate reasons for this development. What has not been brought out is the fact that in these communities where there is the likelihood of young people being drafted and sent to the arena of war, these demonstrations have been very intense. Students of human behaviour have not often emphasised the role that fear of death has played in student demonstrations. Either both young and old alike have repressed the fear of death or there has come into effect a tacit understanding that this existentially crucial matter should not be brought out into the open. Meanwhile the suffering and injustice continue.

It can be seen to be a curious characteristic of the human being that ideas, fears and impulses that he has do find behavioural expression in one way or another. When the not-thinking not-speaking response is operative in regard to an idea, it seems to reach expression in a symbolic form. In some cultures this symbolisation takes the form of rough sports where the vanquished always seem to have to adopt a recumbent posture of inanimation due to the punishment received. In other words one human being seems to be reduced to a state something akin to death. Two different aspects are seen here. The vanquished has symbolically tasted death, sometimes even in a concrete fashion. The victor on the other hand has only had his hypothesis strengthened namely, "one dies but I shall not die". This would lead us to believe that a consistent victor in a rough sport like boxing or free-style wrestling would receive a strengthening of the denial of existential realities like death whereas the 'born loser' would have rehearsals into this forbidden area and would therefore be in a state of Being-for-death. Here symbolism perhaps helps the vanquished but not the victor.

Those in the healing professions particularly the surgeons very often find the phenomenon of death extremely distasteful. The lay public does not properly understand this attitude because it thinks the surgeon being constantly exposed to death among his patients, sometimes unaccountably, should therefore be inured to this contingency. In modern times the doctor has come to be imbued with miraculous powers especially because of the range and variety of chemical agents as also techniques available to him. It is no surprise then that some amount of omnipotence over the living should be invested in the medical practitioner. Most often this remains subliminal but manifests itself as excessive ego-involvement and depressive reactions whenever a patient in his care, dies. At a moderate level of self-awareness this can be seen as an interpretation of professional failure coupled with a fall from omnipotence. In this way the surgeon differs from the psychiatrist or the clinical psychologist in that the latter learns from hard experience that 'cure' is somewhat of a myth in the mental sciences. The plight of the psychiatrist and clinical psychologist is even worse because they have often nothing to give them hope, their feeling of decimation from power being very intense sometimes. At the deepest level, the surgeon perhaps denies his personal vulnerability to death and whenever a patient dies, the latent concept of his immortality receives a vicarious shock. The priest is another person who, despite his constant experience of ministering to the dying, seems to taste of personal annihilation whenever he has to officiate at a funeral. The closer the dead person has had personal relationship with the priest the greater the decimation suffered by the latter. The point of all this is to try to make clear that constant encounter with death need not necessary inure a person against a feeling of terror.

Summary;

It is possible that proper meaning to existence especially when it is of the unfolding kind seems to maintain life, and to remove the terrors of death. This state also makes for an active attitude of Being-for–Death postulated by Heidegger. When meaning is lost which is the same state referred to as an absence of growth unexplained deaths can take place. This kind of death could fall into three categories. In the first, by an act of will the person who has lost his meaning to life opts for death. In the second, he gives up hope and surrenders his will to live. The third category refers to those who again exercise an act of will and by a physical method take their own lives. The first and third categories still have some meaning as the experiencers have chosen to enforce their will, which is the organ of responsibility. Most tragic is the case of the people who fall in the second category as they have relinquished responsibility for their existence. It is possible that some human beings living in situations where others exploit their life force and try to undermine their hope in life with cruel and systematic methodology have the experience of emptiness. Viktor Frankl describes this insidious progression of such a feeling of hopelessness in prisoners of war. He also describes how people in conditions of such dire deprivation have sometimes found an unfolding meaning to their life, which enabled them to survive impossible conditions.

All this seems to make one thing clear. Unspeakable hardships and death itself are experiences that could cause terror, anxiety and panic: but these need not cause emptiness and hopelessness if these experiences have some meaning within the total pattern of existence of the individual. This meaning is a function of awareness and of the willingness of the experiencer to savour both polarities of existence, namely the pleasurable and the unpleasurable.

Therapy—Basic Concepts

Unlike most other schools of psychotherapy the existentially oriented therapist does not normally speak of a rigid system of techniques and postulates. He attempts to interpret the meaning of human experience and in the process delineates a way to a successful living. Basically it is a phenomenological approach that emphasises the thinking, feeling, sensing and acting experiences of the individual as being the cumulative act of existence. To study a human being, the observer cannot merely catalogue a list of readily observable patterns of activity; he has to "feel with" the experiencer and in that way perceive the reality of the subject's experience. To satisfy these requirements the observer has to study the client as a holistic being and not draw inferences from discrete samples of his behaviour, which last would only give a distorted picture of the man.

Secondly, man's relation to society is such that being-with people, in other words having communion with other people, is perhaps the most meaningful way in which individual man's behaviour can be interpreted. Interpretations of being-with-people also seem to differ from culture to culture. In the Western World, this is interpreted to mean active commerce with the people of a society in their day-to-day work and pleasure. In other words, it emphasises a physical togetherness and sharing of experiences. In some other societies as in traditional Hindu societies being-with people is seen to be an evolving concept. To the ordinary man it starts off with physical togetherness and sharing with others around him. With the unfolding of a man's phenomenological world, the concept of being-with people could undergo a change in consonance with the subtlety of inter-human communications. The need for physical proximity could give place to sharing at a deeper level. Whatever be the level of being-with people looked at, it seems that man's greater awareness of himself is not an occurrence in vacuo but one which is the result of some active interaction with other human beings. The greatest fear of man is that of non-being, a sense of personal annihilation. The thesis developed in this book emphasises greater and greater unfolding of self-awareness as a necessary condition for meaningful existence. Sometimes the feelings of emptiness, apathy and lack of meaning to life stem from a non-confrontation of the idea of non-being or various aspects of it. In other words avoidance reactions reduce existential awareness and at the same time diminish a man's contact with the world of people. And with such reduction of awareness comes the experience of anxiety, which is indirectly a measure of man's fear of non-being.

Levels of existence:

Writers on the subject of existence perhaps accept the following convenient classification as a working hypothesis to delineate the levels of ontology.

People whose existence seems to fall predominantly within the level of UMWELT can be said to be living in accordance with the Pleasure Principle described by Freud. Primary drives mainly of a biological nature seem to be forces impelling them to action. And secondly, when these people act, it might be for the satisfaction largely of their immediate primary existence with no clear concepts of teleological orientation. This is considered the lowest state of man, not only because he seeks pleasure predominantly but also because in that state actions performed are not aimed at the creation of greater self-awareness. Secondly existentialists realise more than other people that happiness (pleasure included) cannot be brought about by direct intent but that it is a by-product of certain types of experience.

The category of behaviour falling within the MITWELT includes a person's reactions to significant people in his environment. This means that he has to share meaningful and deep relationships with a person other than himself. The formation of such a significant relationship with another necessitates the vicarious sharing of sensations, thoughts and feelings. The intents (motives) of the individual to act in a specific manner also assume importance. There can be four ways in which man can have his being within the MITWELT. These are referred to as the Modes.

The Anonymous Mode is characterised by lack of differentiation in which the individual effaces his special identity, being content to be one among the crowd.

In the Singular Mode not much of interpersonal relationship is involved.

The Plural Mode refers to relationships in which one individual establishes a system for exploiting those around him without any consideration for the individuality of others. For example, a piece of instrumental behaviour can be an expression of the other person as a significant being whose intimate needs interact with his own; the same piece of behaviour can also be an exploitation of the other if it is carried out without regard to or reference to the experiential needs of the other.

The most desirable one is the Dual Mode in which a person signifies his interpersonal relationships in terms of "we" and "us". This is s system of mutual respect and give-and-take. Such relationships are also exemplified by altruism and a deep emotional involvement that last through all kinds of existential vicissitudes. A relationship that reflects a continuous shared experience at a significant level is referred to in existential psychology as an "Encounter." This is the hallmark of typical, satisfying behaviour within the MITWELT.

The third category known as EIGENWELT is unique in existential psychology and has sometimes been referred to as the quality of "for-me-ness." The constellation of behaviour patterns that can be termed "authentic" refers to that which is in harmony with his habitual self-evaluatory responses. Authenticity goes a little further than concepts like Congruence and Genuineness. According to Bugenthal it is a term used to characterise a way of being in the world in which one's being is in harmony with the being of the world itself. It can therefore be inferred that the greater the self-awareness of the individual the greater his knowledge of his authenticity and his ability to steer his behaviour in conformity with it.

The concept of unfolding awareness is exemplified by the statement "I know something." There are three parts to it, the aspect of the experiencer 'I', the concept of the object 'something' and the link of the subject 'I' with the object 'something' that is represented by the act of knowing. In normal human cognitive exercises it is very seldom these three aspects receive maximal awareness usually one aspect is emphasised at the expense of the others. EIGENWELT perhaps refers to the experience of meaning in its maximal aspect of apprehension.

However it has to be emphasised that Umwelt, Mitwelt and Eigenwelt are not to be seen as necessarily exclusive to one another. (This classification is reminiscent of the three Gunas in Hindu philosophy, namely Tamas, Rajas and Sattwa respectively.) A person has to range over all the three. The greatest portion of his existence that falls in any one category would be expected to determine his level of existence.

Healthy Development of Personality:

Not many existential writings explicitly set forth the attributes and behaviour patterns characteristic of a healthy individual; nor do they delineate ontogenic stages of healthy development. As man is to be studied as a gestalt it would be advantageous to visualise a continuum along which his behaviour patterns could be located. The lower end of this continuum would then represent behaviour characterised by a great deal of disintegrated activity. This stage is also denoted by inadequate differentiation of the personality from environmental forces. The top of the continuum then represents maximal integration of personality that makes for high differentiation and clearer boundaries between the self and external reality. According to this interpretation the development of the individual is an evolutionary process, the developing individual succeeding in bringing more and more areas of his personality into the total integrated system.

Salvadore Madi, an existentialist delineates three aspects to man's nature, which he terms social, biological and psychological. By social he means interpersonal relationships, by biological the physical survival and satisfactions, and by psychological all kinds of mental processes primarily symbolisation, judgment and imagination. Of these three it is the psychological aspect that bestows on man his humanity. He continues: "If you consider yourself bound by certain rules of social interaction on the one hand and in need of certain material goods for satisfaction and survival on the other, relationship between yourself and other people will be made on a contractual basis than on the grounds of tradition or intimacy." When existence becomes a web of contracts, the person becomes a conformist bound by stringent frames of reference. R.W. Emerson says "Whosoever would be a man, must be a non-conformist. A consequence of relying on imagination and judgment as guides to action is that the life of the ideal person would be a frequently changing, unfolding thing."

In an earlier chapter, the concept of the love-gestalt has already been seen as an essential attribute of a person as he essays into the MITWELT. The experiencing person, to be able to fulfil his growth potential to the utmost, becomes progressively aware of more and more constituents of his love-gestalt and can with accuracy emphasise the appropriate ones in every interpersonal relationship.

Mental Disorder:

Within the rationale presented in this book the development of mental illness mainly consists of the inability of the experiencer to become aware of specific areas of his personality. This has two direct consequences. Not becoming aware of certain constituents changes the equilibrium of the system, in itself a homeostatic device towards adjustment, the attempt to create a new gestalt. Secondly, the establishment of a new gestalt means a change in the emphasis of the love-gestalt that may be inappropriate to the relationships entered into by the individual. The altered behaviour resulting from the establishment of a new gestalt and the change in emphasis may be expected to lead to non-authentic response patterns, namely response patterns that do not fit the cognitive system of the experiencing person. The greater the failure of awareness, the larger the areas of the personality, which fail to be represented in the gestalt. This would result in diminished ability of the individual to experience his total existence.

It should be noted that this is not an attempt to simplify the concept of mental illness so that the same basic therapy could be applied to its different manifestations. Nor is this an attempt to play down the value of diagnostic categories especially the two broad divisions of 'functional' mental illnesses which are classed as Psychosis and Neuroses respectively. Existential systems deal with a high degree of differentiation and therefore diagnostic categories which emphasise just-noticeable differences in emotional emphases are accepted within a unified framework. At the same time it has to be remembered that they emphasise gestalt concepts, which means the evolution of economy in explanations. In other words high differentiation is seen as a first step towards integration.

Goals of Therapy:

The main goal of Therapy is the restoration of the ability of the individual to experience his total existence, in other words to enable him to be less of a conformist. The ability to do this is a continuous process. As such, the restoration programme is a graduated one to help the client experience progressively larger areas of his existential potentiality. With greater awareness of his existence he also becomes keenly aware of unpleasurable or distressing experiences. One of the functions of all mental illnesses, in the first instance, seems to be to shut out the awareness of painful or unpleasurable experiences. These are usually psychologically aversive stimuli although they could just as easily be physically noxious ones. The need to assume responsibility, for instance, could be a very noxious internal stimulus for a neurotic person. Therapy, while helping the individual to become more aware of his experiential life, also brings out the capacity of the individual to tolerate some amount of existential suffering. At this stage in therapy the client may be struck by the 'keenness' of his experiential life. This means he enjoys intensely as also suffers deeply depending on which region of his existence he samples. The ultimate goal of therapy is not to make the individual's existence totally pleasurable for that would be an unrealistic aim. When a person can experience existence without shutting out awareness of the external and internal reality, he may well be considered to be on the road to greater integration. In attaining this goal, the therapist may use many methods suited to the individual needs of the client. This does not label him as eclectic in approach although the methods he chooses are varied and are aimed at bringing the client face to face with the reality of existence.

The Therapist:

One of the first requirements for a therapist is perhaps that he should be able to consider his client as a total organism. He has also to have the ability to put himself in the place of his client and to experience vicariously what the latter experiences. This is perhaps the most important aspect of phenomenological approaches to psychotherapy. Communication has to exist at different levels leading to an "encounter' which is a very intimate emotional relationship involving participation between the client and the therapist. In addition to being able to experience with the client at all these levels, the therapist has to be able to be fully aware of the "Dharma" of the relationship. Dharma is a concept from Hindu Philosophy with a multiple significance out of which three are particularly relevant here. Firstly it denotes the ability of a person to take part in existential activities knowing how to distinguish the authentic from the non-authentic. Another aspect of dharma deals with the development of a frame of reference that enables experiences to be undertaken because of their intrinsic value and not because of their expected consequences. The third aspect is that of detachment, the therapist should perhaps be able to experience the encounter in all its intensity as does the client but he has to be detached at the same time. He is both the experiencer and the observer. This change in roles is sometimes alternating; at other times it is simultaneous. The distant goal set for the client is seen as the immediate attribute of the therapist, to be able to experience existential patterns in their kaleidoscopic variety and intensity but without being overcome by the consequences of the act he initiates. The attainment of dharma is the highest stage of existential development.

The requirements for a therapist are thus seen to be very stringent. Natural gifts and predilections for observing the inner life and reality of other phenomenological worlds are essential requisites. Above all, an existential therapist need to have the ability 'to love' human beings in terms of the gestalt concept explained at the beginning of this book. And stemming from the varied qualifications of the therapist mentioned above, it becomes clear that he should be a creative individual who understands strategies of interpersonal relationship. In Existential Therapy rehearsals of life strategies by the client under the supervision of the therapist, are accepted measures.

The Techniques of Therapy:

The aim of existential therapy is to foster in the client three important character-istics, willingness to face existential realities, acquiring the ability to do this and the development of a sense of personal responsibility for his own behaviour. To be able to do all this, the client has to start from humble beginnings. He has to start perhaps with the ubiquitous phenomenon of boredom which plagues human existence. Boredom can be seen as the consequence of restricted cogni-tion, conation and affect. In other words this represents a restriction of existence.

One of the preliminary methods of obviating this would be to start working on the expansion of associations. This is done in a variety of ways. The client is first taught the relaxation of the body and the mind. When he is relaxed he is asked to visualise an object like a flower, for instance. Without making any attempt to hold on to this image or to concentrate on it, the client is required to let pictures flow across his mind and to avoid trying to influence their volume, course or content. A person with conceptual rigidity obviously exercises rigid control over his cognitive processes. This control is not that which can be referred to as purposive direction but which can be termed to be a braking or an inhibi-tion. In the technique referred to here, the object is to enable the client to learn to let go of his control in gradual degrees. By letting images flow across his mind, be these images anxiety-evoking, or positive, or pessimistic or even anti-social, the habitual feeling of restriction is gradually lost. When the mind becomes aware of its freedom and range it is expected that the sense of boredom, which is another way of emphasising dependence on external objects for one's existence, would give way to the ability to feel deeply. It could be that initial essays in this field could conjure up some frightening images. There is also another starting point for associations. This is to start with a physiological response, the beating of the heart or some aspects of breathing. Again without concentrating on the experi-ence but participating in it, the client could enter the realm of his subjective auto-nomic experiences. In other words instead of interpreting his physiological experiences as euphoria, anxiety, tension and so on, the client is encouraged to savour the sensations produced. The ebb and flow of these would then be seen as an essential experiential mode.

Gendlin has advocated a system similar to this based on felt meaning experi-enced by the client. Although existentialists do not make use of the term repres-sion with the same connotation as Freud, they do speak of a condition of reduced awareness or non-awareness of large areas of a client's personality. Many a person who complains of apathy and inability to become interested in anything is merely emphasising his experiential rigidity. By going through exercises in association as explained above, he tries to sample all sorts of experience, pleasurable as well as distressing. The therapist does not merely let the client go away after this exercise. The client tries out his newfound liberty of action in the world at large. It would be expected that pleasure and pain would ensue depending on how the client's behaviour has affected people around him. The therapist and the client at their next meeting look at these consequences. More strategies are generated for the client to rehearse. It would be clear from this, that what the client does is to improve the feedback about his behaviour. Secondly he learns to modulate his behaviour not only towards that which clashes least with that of other people but also to that which satisfies his existence.

Along with these exercises in the levels of meaning, particular experiences of the client, which seem consonant with his self-system, are carefully considered by him and the therapist from various aspects. This process again has the effect of increasing the awareness of the gestalt. Together with the felt meaning of experiences, the power of the word for the client has also a very significant implication. The human organism is different from the lower forms of life in his having an awareness of himself and in his possession of a language. Symbolic verbal behaviour can thus been seen as a consequence of self-awareness. It seems reasonable to assume that greater exercise of symbolic verbal behaviour stems from greater self-awareness. Conversely language provides a very effective channel to modify the degree of self-awareness. In existential therapy therefore it is customary to pay great attention to the "word" and its association. This is not only an intellectual or a semantic exercise but also an emotional one in which the meaning of the word is "felt."

The anti existential pattern of behaviour exhibited by clients includes hostility and fear. From these can be derived attitudes representing aggression and anxiety, all these in turn directed against the world or towards the self. Whatever their manifestation, they all can be seen to stem from fear, the fear of non-being or annihilation. Interpreting this in terms of awareness, it can be said that lack of or inadequate awareness of one's own gestalt pattern of love increases the anticipatory anxiety. The fear of dissolution is again maintained because of avoidance of the idea, an attempt to shut it out from awareness. In existential psychotherapy therefore a client is encouraged to look at the prospect of death, which normally evokes fear or hostility. All these would make it clear that it is the thinking pattern of the client that has to be reorganised. Visualisation of stimulus patterns and full confrontation of these are to be reinstated where avoidance patterns existed before. It should again be emphasised that the concepts of confrontation and the development of strategies carry with them the need for rehearsal. One of the outcomes of rehearsal which also emphasises the gestalt nature of human experience is the fact that any segment of existence can be experienced fully only after several trials. Each essay into real life that the client undertakes is not to be considered in terms of the dichotomous evaluation of success versus failure but only in terms of the area of the gestalt sampled. Thus in different trials, confrontation with the same reality is qualitatively and quantitatively different. However, it is cumulative in that the experiential schemata laid down as a result of previous experiences, alter the further perception of the gestalt and are in turn modified by the successive perception of the latter. Thus in existential terms the concepts of happiness and pain are not static nor are they evoked consistently by the same stimulus pattern. Again, going back to the concept of dharma, successful existence in terms of this interpretation, is the ability to participate in human relationships and corporate social endeavours without these activities having the power to sway the feelings of the experiencer. In other words, existential psychotherapy is aimed at the liberation of the client from excessive field-dependence. The stimulus-bound behaviour of man which result in anxiety is changed to one attuned to phenomenological realities. Erstwhile non-authentic patterns of behaviour are modified into authentic ones.

It would be clear from the above that existential therapy is an individualised method. Every human being to be helped needs techniques of therapy suited to his authenticity, and since existential psychotherapy applies measures aimed at the total rehabilitation of a client, it is essentially a holistic approach. It is aimed at restoring the client's freedom to act in specific ways rather than merely providing him freedom from psychopathology.

A New Technique Of Therapy

Introduction:

Although all systems of therapy deal with anxiety, most of them try to alleviate it by using the content of experiences, relegating affect to a subsidiary role. This chapter describes a therapeutic method, which uses affect to bring about a clearer distinction between pleasant and unpleasant experiences. This seems a little superfluous since most people appear to be able to make this distinction. It is however postulated that in any human experience the predominant feeling tone is the one that decides as to whether it is seen as pleasant or unpleasant. In neuroses the ambivalence is more pronounced, as very often the client is unable or barely able to distinguish this dichotomy in his experiential life. In other words, the more severe the inroads of anxiety into life, the more telescoped pleasant and unpleasant experiences become, resulting in a state of restricted behaviour. The identity crisis that adolescents experience and the lack of meaning to life they report can all be seen aspects of the restriction of experience.

The therapeutic system reported here does not deal directly with the specific contents of experience but uses affect in a unique way so as to produce two distinctly identifiable clusters, one relating to pleasantness and the other to distress. This procedure is basically designed to accomplish a binding of anxiety, to restore to awareness a large number of cognitive as also somatic experiences and to increase the psychological distance between pleasant and unpleasant experiences. Thus without greatly disturbing the thought content, affect is sought to be brought under control. It is expected that in the process greater ability to modulate behaviour would also be achieved.

The basic postulates:

The basic postulates have to do with anxiety because it is seen as the core of the neuroses. Anxiety is neither considered as merely anticipatory fear nor as just conditioned fear. In deriving the rationale used in this method of treatment, anxiety is basically thought to arise on account of the failure of the experiencer to act in accordance with his psychophysiological predispositions. In most neurotic conditions, restriction of the range of behaviour and its stringent inhibition are seen to be the result of failure to distinguish clearly among affective states. Paradoxically the overdriven character of the striving also coexists with inadequate sampling of all the available ranges of behaviour.

The Aims of Therapy:

The following are the broad aims of therapy:

1. Increasing the range of experience.

2. First the enhancement of the ability of the subject to disinhibit his behaviour patterns.

3. To achieve a moving away from the all-or-none pattern of behaviour, in other words, the establishment of voluntary control.

4. Enable the experiencer to distinguish amongst the affective states relating to experiences.

5. Make him aware of the somatic experiences concomitant with cognition, in other words develop the ability to identify somatic data before interpreting them.

6. Achieve a binding of free-floating anxiety.

Details of Therapy:

Imagery:

The first step is to establish the sensory modality of the subject's imagery. Most people are able to imagine visual stimuli but some are also able to enrich this with stimuli from other modalities. The idea of this exercise is to have some baseline data as to the range of stimuli that could cause relaxation. The client is then required to describe in detail five pleasant memories and five distressing ones. The usual practice is to get them to write these down at the outset. The therapist then discusses these with the patient till a very detailed and clear account is available not only of the stimulus complexes represented, but also of their affective connotation.

Relaxation:

Then the client gets training in progressive relaxation which proceeds in two stages. In the first, the patient resting on a comfortable bed is asked to tense and to relax alternately using muscle systems in the lower extremities of the body and then working towards the head. This is similar to the Wolpean technique administered prior to the actual systematic desensitisation in behaviour therapy. In the second stage, the client with his eyes closed is asked to tense up as many muscles as possible all over his body. He is required to do this slowly and gradually not involving any jerking of the muscles. When he feels he has reached the peak of muscular tension he is required to relax, also very slowly and gradually, continuing to do so far beyond the stage at which he feels he has relaxed maximally. The slowness of tensing up and relaxing is considered important in this method because it is hypothesised that this procedure can produce relaxation beyond that usually reported by subjects.

Cognitive disinhibition:

Starting with the initial sessions at relaxation the client is asked not to try to control his thought processes in any way but to let good thoughts or pleasant thoughts or anxiety-evoking thoughts to go across the mind. He is also required not to try to 'control' his body in any way but to let relaxation take its own course. The idea is to accustom the client to a situation of minimal effort. This exercise has been termed cognitive disinhibition because it is aimed at lessening the excessive drive state that characterises most neurotic conditions. Worry, an anxiety-elevating cognitive experience, is usually maintained because of the incessant effort at mastery of the situation constantly conceptualised in imagination. This intensive drive state in turn can be said to produce anxiety. Cognitive disinhibition, by attempting to take away the rigid framework within which repetitive neurotic thought operates, enables perception to disappear from awareness or come back without the ritualism present in repetitiveness. It must be made clear that cognitive disinhibition is not seen as an end in itself but only as a step in releasing neurotic thought processes from their repetitive character. The sequence of events can be conceptualised as disinhibiton, later development of facile control of thought processes and the ability to modulate them according to volition.

Exercises which help in Cognitive Disinhibition:

Performing some exercises can accelerate the disinhibition of thought processes.

1. The client can be requested to focus attention on a physiological behaviour pattern like breathing. He is asked to watch his own breathing as an observer and not to attempt its modification in any way. It is usually found that this procedure results in the breathing becoming deeper and slower. The observation of breathing constitutes transference of attention from cognitive phenomena and could result in disinhibiting thought processes.

2. Another exercise requires the subject to relax, close his eyes and to visualise as clearly as possible a lighted candle on a candlestick. When the imagery is very clearly evoked, he is asked to indicate the fact by raising his little finger. Then the therapist asks him to remove the candlestick from his imagery. Later the image of the candle is removed in the same way leaving only the flame. And then finally the flame also. The state of awareness that is left is reported by many subjects as being without thought or images. This state apparently can only be held for very brief periods.

    Among other images amenable to such progressive ablation are a long stemmed rose in a tall vase, and a long stemmed lotus flower. It must be clear now that almost any image capable of being visualised can lead to the state described above.

Affective Constancy:-

The next step is the one dealing specifically with the affect. The subject is relaxed, given a few minutes to exercise cognitive disinhibition and then asked to visualise one of the five pleasant experiences he had described at the outset. On visualising such an experience a pleasant affect is evoked. When the subject feels that the affect has been optimally evoked, he signals that fact by raising his little finger. The therapist then requests him to hold the affect constant and to let his attention range over memories of past events that have had a similar affective connotation. During this "scanning" which occurs in a state of cognitive disinhibiton, the attention of the subject is mainly directed towards the holding of the affect constant. But this is not to say that fluctuations do not occur; usually subjects report changes in intensity of the affect. With this continued exercise there occurs a "clustering effect"–the binding together of memories having similar pleasant affective connotations. Thereafter evocation of the pleasant affect relating to one such memory beings in a cumulative affect usually resulting in an accentuation of the feeling tones. This exercise can be repeated over very many sessions thus enhancing the number of elements in the cluster.

Then an unpleasant memory is dealt with in the same way. Care is taken however to see that the distressing affect evoked, is not too intense as to constitute a trauma. Therefore, out of the five memories of unpleasant events the least noxious is chosen.

On optimal evocation of distress the client signals this fact. Thereupon he is requested to focus attention on the unpleasant affect and let his awareness range over other memories of events which may have led to a similar affect. Again a "clustering" of unpleasant memories takes place around the nucleus of the distressing affect. This constitutes the binding of anxiety. This exercise is also continued over many sessions resulting in adding many more elements to the cluster. Sometimes it happens that a client would be unable to tolerate this procedure with equanimity for a long period of time. Whenever this happens, the exercise with pleasant memories and the affect of joy is undertaken alternately with the distressing one.

A Paradoxical Effect:

A paradoxical effect is seen in this type of therapy. The pleasant affect seems to increase in intensity both during the sessions and in real life on coming across a pleasant experience.

The distressing affect is seen to decrease in intensity during the therapeutic sessions. However the person seems to "suffer" more on encountering unpleasant experiences that did not evoke such sensitivity before therapy. In other words the keenness of affect is increased in both pleasant and unpleasant areas.

Assumptions made:-

The following basic assumptions have been made in initiating this therapeutic system:

1. Everyone can probably learn to relax and to disinhibit his cognitive processes.

2. It is possible to "observe" a somatic experience without trying to modify it wittingly.

3. It is possible to hold an affect without attending to the visualisation of its context.

4. A clustering effect can be made to take place around a constantly held affect, attracting ideas and images with similar affective connotations.

5. That when the image and its unpleasant affect are associated, the phenomenon of binding of anxiety takes place.

6. The binding of anxiety is therapeutic and diminishes the distress of the client.

7. There are qualitative differences in the experience of anxiety.

Possible explanation of the therapeutic effects:

1. Some of the associated situations causing the same quality of unpleasant affect may have occurred in the historical past of the individual and do not constitute threatening stimuli any more. By linking the present affect to situations that have ceased to be anxiety evoking to the experiencer, some of the current pathological anxiety is reduced.

2. Unpleasant affect, if held constant and looked at objectively seems to result in habituation and consequent reduction in intensity. It is possible that desensitisation takes place.

3. Awareness of the anxiety of situations which have produced similar affect in the past breaks the connotation of its special nature. This "special-nature" effect is often a factor in the perpetuation of neurotic anxiety.

Case Studies

1. The Child Wife:

Mrs. C. an attractive 20-year old, was referred to a Psychiatric Unit by her general practitioner. The presenting symptoms were difficulty with sleep, constant sensations of nausea and frequent bouts of crying. The last was an alarming sign in that not only would the crying give her no relief but it would also sometimes become difficult to stop it. Her husband, about ten years older, a very extraverted businessman went through stages of irritation, annoyance, hostility and finally alarm at the apparently meaningless pattern of behaviour his wife evinced. On admission into the comparatively secure environment of the psychiatric ward, Mrs. C's symptomatology suddenly seemed to clear up. Only a week after admission and close observation, her psychiatrist decided that her problems concerned fundamental aspects of her style of life. In other words he was convinced that she was a person whose emotional growth patterns and abilities for sophisticated interpersonal encounters were those of a young child. She had to learn innumerable strategies and grow up into a purposeful adult human being. He rightly estimated that this could take a long time. The small psychiatric unit was hardly the place where this intensive ego restructuring could be attempted. At this point, she was referred to the author for existential therapy on an outpatient basis.

From the beginning it was found that the client would form a very dependent relationship with the therapist; she seemed to seek approval for everything she did; indeed she continued to ask him what she should do with her life.

Her life story up till then presented an array of sub-threshold and supra-threshold traumata that had built up slowly and had resulted in her breakdown. She was the second of two children, both girls. Her father, a civil servant, suffered a neurotic breakdown during the Second World War and had to be repatriated from active duty overseas. Ever since then he had been preoccupied with his own problems and consequently he had little time for his family. His wife sheltered the husband on the one hand from being disturbed by the two young children and the latter from being shouted at or being punished by their father. Ever since her own marriage, she had developed migraine headaches for which she received physical and psychological treatment. The two children had an age difference of about two years. The older girl was always considered fragile by her mother who explicitly and implicitly gave credence to the stereotype that she was a very sensitive child who needed to be handled with kid gloves. The younger one (later to become Mrs. C) was always considered a stolid child slow to cry and, it seemed, able to withstand the occasional punishments the parents meted out to her. It seemed also that she had a will of her own. While talking about her childhood Mrs. C remembered having strong feelings that injustice had been done to her and of jealousy towards her elder sister who seemed to have received the lion's share of her parents' affection. The result was a gradual development of perception of parental rejection and of her own self as being worthless. The parents, of Roman Catholic persuasion, were strict about the need for religious observances on the part of their two children. The younger child, when she was 7 years of age took her first communion. She distinctly remembered the adulation of her relatives whose comments about how exquisitely pretty she looked in her white dress, were like delicious food and drink. Her pleasure was short lived in that during the ceremony she became very nervous and for the first time suffered acute sensations of nausea and giddiness. Thereafter whenever she found herself stressed in any way she would develop these symptoms. Her earliest memory that intruded into her anamnestic accounts was that of being slapped by her father repeatedly when she was only three years of age. She also recollected the anger, shame and humiliation she felt then. Despite these overwhelming emotions she did not cry on being punished but maintained a brave front. Her relationship with her mother had always been ambivalent consisting of intense needs for dependency coupled with hostility and aggression. The overt and implicit preference for her older sister by her mother seemed to increase with the passing years. The younger daughter, despite her attractive appearance and the apparent ability to withstand stressful situations, found her self-esteem progressively diminishing. One of the outcomes was her somewhat submissive relationship towards young men. She was about 17 when she had her first boy friend. Although in the beginning he was very attentive to her, he seemed to change as their relationship progressed. He became demanding and while with other young people, he neglected her completely. All this time there was no sexual relationship involved. Finally her boy friend tried to force her to acquiesce to his sexual demands, whereupon she went into a panic and broke off her relationship with him. This stormy, ambivalent and unsatisfactory relationship with its abrupt termination seemed to have a peculiar effect on her. Instead of having an effect of caution on her, she seemed to think that she had to throw herself on the first comer so that she could at least have the satisfaction of knowing she had a steady boy friend. Thereafter she submitted to sexual activity with her boyfriends. The last one in the series of three was he who became her husband. Although they had only occasional sexual relations, this young man was throughout attentive and considerate towards her, and for the first time she felt a person in her own right. Finally the day of the wedding was fixed. Her troubles started anew. She had attacks of panic, nausea and giddiness. The general practitioner who saw her prescribed tranquillisers. One her wedding day she was so heavily drugged that her consciousness of the proceedings became very blurred. At one point she even thought she wouldn't be able to go through with it. After the wedding the symptoms seemed to get aggravated. The new one was the tendency to have frequent bouts of uncontrollable crying. For some time she tried to go out with her husband on his business trips in a bid to avoid being alone. But she felt that her unhappiness was making him irritable. It was at this time she came for treatment. Then she was bride of only a few months.

She underwent many psychological tests. She was seen to function at the lower reaches of the normal range in so far as her cognitive abilities were concerned. Her concept formation operated at a concrete level. On some of the projective tests and questionnaires, her protocols generally indicated a high level of anxiety, immaturity in social relationships and non-productive aspect of her intelligence. She also appeared to have an intelligence complex which made for an inordinate desire to present herself at all times in the best possible light. Her level of intellectual sophistication appeared to be exceptionally low. It would become clear from this account that almost every aspect of Mrs. C's life would be looked upon as a problem. Among the many therapeutic aims that could be postulated, the following seemed to be urgent.

1. Reduction of anxiety connected with many aspects of her life

2. The raising of her self-esteem

3. Increasing the range of her life experiences

4. Helping her relinquish excessive efforts at coping with life

5. Generating adequate strategies to cope with life situations and rehearsing them.

6. Helping her to realise her own authenticity.

One of the very first things done in the therapeutic setting was to generate strategies to deal with three types of interpersonal relationship, the one with her mother, with her husband and with her friends or acquaintances. The relationship with her mother had always been ambivalent but at the time of commencing treatment, Mrs.C had an understanding to have lunch with her mother once a week, followed by an afternoon of shopping. The mother's presence was always something of a damping experience with her. Most of the talking at these encounters seemed to be done by the mother. In the therapy sessions, ways of overcoming the inhibitions were looked at. Topics, which Mrs.C. was adept at, were worked out. She then tried to put these into practice when she was actually with her mother. The rehearsal of strategies was particularly helpful in increasing her sales resistance. Whereas formerly she would buy things she didn't want, she was able later on to resist even persuasive salesmen. This ability raised her self-esteem considerably. She was then able to discuss her resentments very frankly with her mother. The latter was somewhat nonplussed about the sudden manifestation of independence on Mrs. C's part. At this time the father seemed to move in her favour, which again could have been due to her altered perception of him. The therapist has met Mrs. C's mother and father a few times. Both have been to psychiatrists and psychologists. Their attitude towards psychological treatment was definitely prejudiced. However, they both promised to be a little more demonstrative of their affection towards their younger daughter and they agreed to support her in her search for self-esteem.

As mentioned before, Mrs. C's life was full of problems. It is not possible to give a blow-by-blow account of all these and the way they were overcome, but a few representative ones will be dealt with here to illustrate the general nature of the therapy. One of her earliest interpersonal problems concerned the expression of assertiveness. To give an example. She belonged to a tennis club to which her mother also went of an afternoon. Mrs. C was a fairly good player and very soon joined up with three other girls of her age group. One of these girls who very often partnered her was a blunt loud spoken person who would always ask Mr. C. to retrieve the tennis balls whenever they fell outside the fencing. The latter would, without question acquiesce. On discussing these incidents with the therapist, Mrs.C. would pour out her deep sense of hurt that her partner would get her to do these chores and order her about. While she would boil with anger inside, she was unable to express it or to refuse the demands of her partner. Strategies were worked out in the therapeutic context. Mrs. C. decided to express her unwillingness next time this happened. When her partner demanded that she retrieve the ball, she was able to say quietly that she had done her share and would her partner run after the ball! The other girl appeared somewhat surprised but quietly retrieved the ball. This would seem a very small step but this demonstrated to Mrs. C. that she could be assertive in a polite way and that no dreadful consequences or rows would necessarily follow. She later struck up a very meaningful friendship with her tennis partner.

At about this time she felt well enough to take up a part-time job as a hairdresser in a salon. Mrs. C. had had some training in this field before her marriage. The owner of this establishment could be described as a middle-aged, sour lady who seemed to pick on Mrs.C. and to make the latter's life miserable. Here again Mrs. C. was unable to assert herself in a meaningful way. The best she could do was to throw a temper tantrum, which only emphasised her helplessness. Again strategies were generated and rehearsed in the therapeutic situation. She was able to apply these successfully at work. She then made the rather startling discovery that her boss suffered from great feelings of inadequacy and lack of meaning to life. Mrs. C. was able to feel compassion for the older woman, which again resulted in a lasting friendship.

At about this time, this client had to have elaborate work done on her teeth that would require a couple of months with weekly sessions. The knowledge of this made her panic. It was not the pain involved in the operation that made her flinch; it was some intangible element in the whole situation that caused her distress. The possible ways of overcoming this were discussed with the client and systematic desensitisation was decided upon as the therapy of choice. Mrs. C, proved to be able to relax quite well, sometimes she spontaneously went into a hypnotic trance. A fear hierarchy was prepared and the desensitisation was begun. There was almost an immediate carryover of therapeutic effects into the dentist's surgery; soon she was able to go there by herself, await her turn without getting anxious and sometimes undergo painful drilling work on her teeth without anaesthetic. This gave her greater confidence in her ability towards self-control.

The client by this time had come a long way in the art of successful living and she decided that she would like to learn to drive the car. Her husband who used to take his van on his business round thought this would be an excellent idea, as the car was mostly standing idle in the garage. He attempted to teach his wife, but his impatience and annoyance at her ineptitude seem to rouse in her again a sense of worthlessness. However, she refused to give up the attempt and at the therapist's idea decided to enrol in a driving school. Very soon she mastered the art and applied for the test. She suffered some anxiety before the test but this was dispelled through systematic desensitisation. To her surprise and delight she passed at the first attempt.

Although the client had progressed very satisfactorily in all areas of her existence there were some complex issued connected with her relationship to her husband, which needed attention. She felt for instance that her husband needed her
body only for his gratification without satisfying her intense need for romance.
The husband appeared a matter of fact person who was even less sophisticated
than his wife. They both were requested at the outset to read a good book on the
sexual adjustments required in marriage. Some combined sessions were held, in
which very frank discussions took place. These did not merely refer to their marriage but they also concerned various existential matters. The author belongs to
an Eastern culture that differed somewhat on several aspects from the Western
culture. But the intermingling of three phenomenological worlds, hers, his and
the therapist's was a remarkable experience in human understanding. Without in
any way adopting conscious strategies, the husband and wife were able to make a
happy adjustment to their mutual needs. Two last problems remained.

The first concerned the difference of opinion between the husband and wife
about starting a family. Mr. C. wanted to have children urgently because he felt
he was growing older and he couldn't afford to wait any longer. She, on her part,
was terrified at the impending responsibility which raising a child would entail.
She was also afraid of losing her figure, of being 'tied down' and of being unable
to go to parties. More than anything she was terrified at the pain of childbirth.
She said that when she felt completely well she would have no objection whatsoever about having a baby. Systematic desensitisation together with rehearsing of
various strategies resulted in being able to face the prospect of having a family.
She then adopted another defence. What if the therapist were leave the country
and go overseas? What if she, after having a baby broke down and needed help?
This last self-deluding defence was looked at carefully and alternatives considered.

A date was set for her to discontinue her visits for therapy. She left the shelter
of the therapeutic encounter willingly and happily. Altogether 96 weekly sessions
over a period of 2 years were required to bring the therapy to a successful conclusion.

There is a sequel to this. Mr. C met the therapist accidentally a year and a half
after his wife stopped her therapeutic sessions. He proceeded to say that his wife
was expecting a baby and that she was coping well with her pregnancy. After the
baby was born, things seemed to go well for a time. Then for no reason at all, or
so it seemed to Mrs.C., she began have bouts of crying and to feel that she
wanted to hurt the baby. She seemed to have the classical symptoms of postnatal
depression. Her distress became so great that she had to be hospitalised. While in

hospital the therapist saw her regularly and her husband sometimes. Her difficulties revolved around the baby. Mainly these were connected with the oppressive sense of responsibility that she felt "trapped". The baby had to be looked after and she would have no life of her own. This would not be for a short time but it would be till the baby grew at least into adolescence. Mrs. C's problem was anticipatory anxiety. Like most people having intense anxiety, Mrs. C also lived in the future instead of living from day to day with the problems cut down to size. Part of this anticipatory anxiety was reduced by systematic desensitisation. For the rest, she was encouraged to look at the situation as it was, instead of trying hard to avoid it. At first her distress seemed to increase in intensity but she persevered. This was really hard work for a person unaccustomed to facing problems head on. The distress decreased progressively. Within two weeks she was able to go home. She continued her visits to the therapist once a fortnight for two months at the end of which she decided she would like to cope with bringing up the baby by herself without having to rely on therapeutic help. Six months later she rang up to say that she would like to come back for just one session. She brought her baby son too and it was obvious from her radiant appearance that she was learning to cope with life's problems. She was very attentive towards the son without undue fuss. The question that she asked was naïve one; she wanted to know whether it was advisable for her to have another baby. She wished to have an assurance that if she had another she wouldn't go into a distressful situation as she did before. To a person unfamiliar with her erstwhile infantile behaviour patterns, this query would come as a bewildering one, but it only showed her tendency to abrogate responsibility for her actions and to invest an external authority with power to advise. In one way this unsophisticated enquiry was a good thing in that it provided a good starting point for looking at models and strategies. During the encounter which ensued, she was able to perceive how she was trying to avoid responsibility. The therapist does not believe in clinical detachment; he does not also believe that the client should not be given advice. But in the present situation he felt that Mrs. C. had come a long way from what she was a few years ago. She had developed more sophisticated and complex cognitive behaviour patterns. She agreed that it was difficult for another person to predict what her behaviour would be a few months hence. She agreed that she herself should assume responsibility for actions. The therapist has not seen Mrs. C. for a few months but her husband rang up to say that everything was going extremely well and that Mrs. C. appeared to be a new person. It is true Mrs. C. had come a long way from her naiveté; but she still had to attain greater insight into her mental processes. This is seen as an unfolding process and the writer is aware that there could be occasions in the future when Mrs. C. might seek his assistance. This is not seen as a relapse but only as a stage she has to go through in her struggles to actualise her potential.

2. The Esoteric Family:

This family consists of three members, the mother Mrs. D, the elder son Paul aged 21 years and the younger Ronald aged 19 years. The youngest member first. The author had known Ronald for a period of a year and a half before he requested therapy. The first encounter with Ronald in a non therapeutic situation was when his girl friend who was undergoing therapy with the author brought him along to give more 'inside information' on her behaviour pattern. At that time he had beautiful wavy hair brushed back neatly and he was wearing a smart suit. Even on that occasion the author noticed two things about this young man, that he tended to be a predominantly divergent thinker and that he was inclined towards esoteric persuasions. The girl had completed therapy and some time had elapsed before Ronald rang up the author suddenly and requested an interview. He explained his reasons for seeking this interview in the following terms. He had given up the use of drugs like marijuana some months before. Since then his life had become empty. He had the feeling of having lost something. His self-esteem was very low and the awareness of his inadequacies overpowering.

During the first interview his fantasy life was explored thoroughly to establish two things, his predominant imagery pattern and to see which themes he resorted to in order to achieve relaxation. He spoke at length about his experiences under the influence of marijuana. This drug seemed to provide him with insights to carry on his interpersonal relationships with some degree of success. He eventually gave it up because he disliked the artificiality of his existence with the need to boost up his experiences constantly with that prop. Ronald was a very good subject for relaxation. Therefore he was asked to furnish clear accounts of a few distressing experiences and of a few joyous ones. The surprising thing was that he couldn't furnish clear accounts of either. He explained his failure to do so as being due to his inability to experience meaningful joy or meaningful suffering. To him all these experiences had a diffuse emotional quality hard to specify and categorise. In other words what he was trying to explain was that his experiential range had become very narrow. The intermediate gaol of therapy was to increase this range so that joyful events would engender more intense pleasurable affect and the distressing ones more painful affect. The keenness of experiencing had to be intensified. Two experiences with clear pleasurable affect were that of going to a dance with some particular friends and enjoying himself at the beach. Using both these imaginary situations, the client when relaxed was required to raise his left index finger when the pleasurable affect could be clearly experienced. Then he was requested to keep the affect steady but to let the mind wander. This resulted in the bringing into memory of other experiences that may have caused similar states of affect. He was able to remember many forgotten and half-forgotten incidents that gave him pleasure in the past. Within a couple of sessions of this kind of practice Ronald reported a gradual dawning of his interest in life. He began to be able to want to do small things that had given him pleasure before. The items representing great distress and suffering were also hard for him to remember. It was decided therefore to make use of his generalised sense of inadequacy and distress as the stimulus for visualisation. This proved to be hard for the patient to do, particularly as this was the very thing he strenuously sought to avoid, but he agreed to do this. His subjective report later made it clear that the painful affect was clearly felt when he was asked to hold the affect constant and to let his mind range over other events from the past with similar connotations. He was able to recall fairly vividly some of his experiences. At the end of that session he had felt the keenness of his distress not as an all-pervasive dull pain but as intense suffering. In this way his range of feeling was extended gradually. He continued to report intenseness of joys and the sharp pain of unpleasant experiences. His spontaneity seemed to increase. It was at this time that he started reporting many dreams, most of them in colour. Some of these dreams were frightening, others having a connotation of anxiety but a few were pleasant ones. He got himself a job as a building labourer. The physical exercise he saw as an exhilarating thing. His interest in religion and his enquiry into matters concerning life and death seemed to come alive suddenly. He found satisfaction in reading books of an esoteric nature and in attending discourses on philosophy. His studies of a very specialised but on-the-fringe topic received a fresh impetus and he spent all his leisure time reading. It might be interesting to an analyst to note that when all these things were happening to him, Ronald felt the full impact of his animosity towards his elder brother on many counts, some of them rational, others irrational. One of Ronald's deep-seated resentments was that his brother had prevented his spontaneous development into an autonomous adult, he having overwhelmed his younger brother. Even the sight of the room in which his brother lived seemed to cause him distress. This was overcome by systematic desensitisation. His relationship towards his mother also underwent a change for the better in that Ronald seemed all of a sudden to appreciate his mother's concern for her children and also to empathise with her aspirations. This client has concluded therapy. At the time of writing 20 weekly sessions have been completed. Ronald has still his moments of despair but he snaps out of them quickly.

Paul was somewhat of an infant prodigy from all that the mother has to say. He was bright in his early schooling and he seemed to breeze his way with flying colours without really trying. However he was a frail little boy with his golden hair almost down to his shoulders. Both these things made him somewhat of a target for fun in the eyes of his friends. Like Shelley he was tormented by his schoolmates who liked to call him a sissy. Despite Paul's renunciation of force as a coercive medium, he stood his ground with great courage. All this made his school life miserable. When he was 14, due to sheer accident, a prominent artist saw his paintings, recognised their potential and recommended him for a scholarship to study art. Paul's work was admired and his teachers held out a career of great promise for him. It was at this time that an event of great significance occurred. Paul was travelling with his companions in a car which had seen better days. An accident occurred. No one in the group seemed seriously hurt but Paul thought he had hurt his back. He was in some pain which went away after a few weeks. But a strange transformation seemed to have occurred in his personality. His usual indefatigable drive seemed almost non-existent. He lay in bed for long periods of time preoccupied with his thoughts or just being in a twilight state of existence. He got up only to eat. He lost interest in his appearance and almost always looked unkempt and wild. A little later he gathered together a few friends of both sexes with the same kind of lotus-eater outlook on life as his own. These young people played the guitar and sang or held esoteric discussions which were of a high level of abstraction. His mother also told me of wild parties they had in the home of one of their number. At these parties they smoked marijuana and sometimes even tried LSD. Paul claimed later that he obtained some kind of intuitive understanding of the world, internal and external, as a result of these trips into the psychedelic unknown; and what is more, he also claimed that some of these flashes of understanding carried over into the realm of normal mental working. This last claim has not usually been substantiated by regular users of the hard drugs who always find that brilliant aspects of enlightenment disappear subtly as the effects of the drug wear off. Drugs did alienate his sense of frustration to some extent, but confusion reigned in his mind at other times. The distress that Paul felt then was a combination of some amount of physical pain, a sense of desolation, absence of meaning to life and an acute feeling of misery. In a sense Paul's life could be referred to as one devoid of direction. This made him try many things. Finally he came to know an osteopath whose esoteric knowledge first intrigued Paul and then fascinated him. This man persuaded Paul that his condition was due to the faulty alignment of C1, and that gradual manipulation and massage of the top of his spine would ease his condition and make for clarity of mind. Paul had had innumerable sessions with the osteopath. Immediately after a session, he feels vastly improved. His thoughts seem to clear and his motivation towards living to improve. Unfortunately these moments of clarity were not only short-lived but also few and far between. It was Paul's brother tho first broached the subject of his coming to therapy with the author. When he first turned up for therapy he was rather wary. His attitude was: "I have tried them all. They do good for sometime but then I am back to my state of confusion." However he formed a meaningful rapport with the author who was able to discuss with Paul some of the relevant points of interest in Indian philosophy especially relating to problems of meaning and the value of suffering. At each session maximal relaxation training was attempted. His range of experience also was sought to be expanded using similar techniques as the ones used with Ronald. Paul was a good subject for relaxation and this fact coupled with his capacity for very vivid visualisation made for very deep states of muscular relaxation. He reported very vivid hypnagogic phenomena not of the world of people but of strange and exotic scenes. He saw these in very attractive colours. His aesthetic sense was so pronounced and his visualisation so realistic that sometimes when he was asked to picture a cave with crystal formations he expressed irritation at the sharpness of the crystal edges. With Paul the trouble was not perhaps about the keenness of his experiential perception but rather the overwhelming nature of his hopelessness. This in turn was the result of his knowledge that his motivation and also his creativity were at a low ebb. The pressing nature of his complaint was his desperate need to recapture the richness of his pre-accident existence. Existential therapy consisting of sampling in visualisation and in real life as many diverse experiences as possible with pleasurable or unpleasurable affects, over a period of time seemed to restore his motivation for two things, namely the longing to be able to paint again and the need to get a job. He began to turn his hand to paining. Later he got a job in a nightclub playing the guitar part of the time and doing other chores the rest of the time. At about this time he discontinued therapy saying that he was too tired doing so many things at the same time. In terms of existential therapy the outcome can be considered as encouraging. Paul's mother still keeps in touch with the writer occasionally. She, however, thinks that Paul has not made any great advance over his previous condition.

The mother of Ronald and Paul (Mrs. D.) requires special mention because of her intense striving to understand not only her sons but also adolescents in general. Although she was not in therapy with the writer, he has interviewed her once. The construction of her personality profile, sketchy as it is, is through the eyes of her sons. Mrs. D. enjoyed bringing up her sons till that awful tragedy overtook her in which she lost her husband and later lost Paul in his mood of existential aberration. Her native intellectual sophistication and esoteric interests did not receive any encouragement so long as her husband was alive. She was then content to bask in the vicarious sunshine of her sons' achievements. But with the trauma came a period of utter hopelessness. She went on a pension and descended from gloom to despair. The maladaptive behaviour patterns of both her sons did very little to alleviate her condition. At one point she went on an extended tour of Europe. She tried osteopathy; she tried faith healing; she tried Krishnamurthi's philosophy; she tried Yoga. Not one of these by itself helped her greatly but it extended her range of interests and experience. It convinced her that the solution to her problems lay within her and in her ability to assume responsibility for her life and that of her children. With dawning realisation of this truth came her phenomenal striving. She coaxed, cajoled, threatened, hated, loved, pushed, pulled and jarred her sons into action. She tried out her strategies and ideas with a boldness born out of surrender, the feeling that too much of effort could sometimes backfire. She understood surrender not as a passive acquiescence but as a dynamic open-mindedness akin to acceptance of all existential experiences despite their varying feeling tones. At the time of writing she continues her esoteric pursuits of reading, listening, loving and experiencing. She does not seem easily put down. Her native resilience makes her come up after every storm. It is hard to say how much is her own strength and how much she owes to the testing of her strategies in her sons' lives, vicariously. The therapist here acknowledges freely the enrichment of his life as a result of knowing this esoteric family.

3. The alienated Young man in search of Love:

One would think 21 is a significant year in one's life. It was not so for Martin the second son amongst three brothers and a sister. His eldest brother was perhaps the only one among the siblings who was, in the eyes of the world, a success. Martin's father a successful businessman always considered himself and was considered by others, to be an uncomplicated person who appeared phlegmatic. He did not seem to be affected by the vicissitudes of life but went about his business calmly. A man of fixed habits, his days were full with little time for regrets. In course of time he acquired his own house and a modest nest egg. The mother in contrast, could be termed to be highly strung. She had a part-time job especially to help her pass the time. The children were grown up and there wasn't much she could do in the house during the day. She was proud of her husband and her home, but somewhat disappointed in her children. But she did try to apportion her love impartially to everyone; in fact it seemed as if her love was so inexhaustible that she revelled in offering it. The children seemed to reciprocate these feelings. The second son, Martin, seemed to be the exception. He thrived on his parents' affection well into adolescence. His mother noticed that Martin, from his childhood was always a "well-behaved' boy who never disobeyed his parents; nor did he get into pranks. He was a good sportsman. Early adolescence seemed to change him somewhat; he seemed to withdraw more and more into himself. The reason for this withdrawal from active commerce with his environment was such a gradual process that not many people were aware of what was happening. The religious practices of this family are rather important to the study. The parents have always been very conscientious Catholics and Martin as a young lad was an Altar boy. It is probable that the dawn of adolescent sexual awakening also brought some conflicts with it. These were to be brought to light later on in the boy's life. Martin had wet dreams during this time and this made him think he was a bad Catholic. He also seems to have felt debilitated after these dreams.

He came to be referred to the writer through a colleague who had known the family for a number of years. Martin had before then been treated by a psychiatrist for a couple of years for a psychotic breakdown. The aloofness that the family had noticed in him from adolescence came to a head. Nevertheless Martin had a very attractive girl friend with whom he was going steady. He finally decided to take the plunge, proposed to the girl and was accepted. The girl wore his ring as became a fiancée. Martin's real troubles began from then on. Both he and the girl indulged in somewhat intense petting behaviour. She wanted him very often to fondle her breasts. He obliged but found a strange intensification of his guilt feeling, with attendant anxiety. After each such encounter with his fiancée he would go into prolonged bouts of silent withdrawals. Some hallucinatory behaviour also became apparent then. Neither the parents nor his betrothed could understand his agitation, which they put down to pre-wedding nerves. Suddenly for no apparent reason, Martin broke off his engagement and told the girl he never wanted to see her again. The poor girl was distraught but there was nothing that anyone could do to change Martin's mind. His hallucinatory activity became intensified. At this stage he was referred to a psychiatrist. It is interesting to note that all the while he held down a technical position with tolerable success. The customary anti-psychotic drugs were administered with an immediate improvement becoming apparent. Within a few months he was slowly back to the original state of bizarre experiences. It was then that the writer came to know him first. The client was first advised not to give up the antipsychotic drugs but to continue them as prescribed by the psychiatrist. The idea was to reduce the dosage when he showed signs of improvement and of better ability to cope with life.

The immediate problems that Martin brought with him were precisely formulated which in itself was rather interesting, usually patients with the type schizophrenic breakdown Martin had would be hard put to, to enunciate their difficulties. Martin's were:

- His constant masturbation and resultant guilt feelings.

- His loneliness and inability to make friends especially of the opposite sex.

- Whenever he chanced to take a girl out, the girl's desire for heavy petting always resulted in his acquiescence but subsequent feelings of guilt and depression.

- His ambivalent feelings towards his parents.

- His resentment at having to take drugs over a long period of time.

It was agreed that client would see the therapist once a week early in the morning, at 8, before he went to work.

From the beginning it was evident that the decline in self-esteem he had experienced probably as a result of his maladaptive relationships with other people was one of his main problems. He had always felt that people were using him for their own purposes. This applied not only to his own family but also to his friends especially his girl friends. Although he played games like cricket and baseball regularly, his muscles remained tensed up most of the time. Therapy was begun with emphasis on the following:

- Physical relaxation

- Imaging of holistic pictures of pleasant life experiences.

- Discussion and evolution of life strategies

- The testing and evaluation of these strategies.

The first two of the above steps presented some difficulty and a few sessions were needed to get him relaxed properly. Thereafter the improvement was rapid. The strategies of life were developed particularly in a graduated way. The tasks he set himself to do were very simple ones to start with. For instance, one of these had to do with his lunch break. He found the one-hour interval away from work somewhat irksome because he felt there was nothing he could do then. His colleagues played cards but Martin had a belief that playing cards was difficult, probably sinful too. He decided to watch his companions playing and he realised that the skill as also concentration required for this activity was not very great. Finally he was persuaded to play. He was pleased to find that he could hold his own in this game of skill. This also had the effect of filling his lunch hour and of drawing him out of his self-imposed alienation from his companions. The next problem to be tackled concerned his relationship with his family. He envied his father's 'lack of problems' and his seeming contentment with life. Although his father took Martin to his club of an evening to have a beer with the 'boys', the latter remained rather anxious and tense in his encounter with older men. True these visits gave him a sense of companionship with his father, but this alone was not considered worthwhile enough to continue them. Martin discussed this aspect with the writer and for the first time he brought out the possibility as to how he and his father were both playing a game denying from each other their fears about the futility of this gesture. His father seemed to feel "obliged" to take his son to the club and be good to him although this was a great strain. Martin, on the other hand felt "obliged" to accept his father's invitation only because the latter would be hurt otherwise. In this way both were showing non-authentic ways of behaviour for their respective existential modes. Martin was able to talk this over with his father, who was very understanding. This talk also seemed to relieve the father considerably. Martin was able to suggest to his father that while he was grateful for these invitations he would accept them only when he felt equal to facing his father's friends. At other times his father was not to feel hurt. This small but significant encounter seemed to lead to greater spontaneity of behaviour between father and son.

At this time there was a little 'trouble" between Martin and his mother; the latter described her son as being tight-fisted and of resenting her request that he raise the money he paid for board to a more meaningful level. Martin thought the request unreasonable as he was a son and that the parents had a duty towards him. This was a difficult point to overcome because Martin had rationalised his stand on a number of counts. For one thing his need to "hoard" money was a bit of a compulsion with him especially as he liked to feel "secure." For another, he was rather confused as to his overt physical dependence on his family. The therapist was assisted greatly by the cooperativeness of the mother who was prepared to wait and to have 'encounters' with her son as to the 'duties' involved in being a mother and in being a son respectively. The writer considered the payment of

increased board only as a symbol of deeper issues involving the child-parent relationship. It was felt that the issue being crucial to the existence of Martin, it
should not be forced at all. At every weekly therapeutic session some reference to
this would come up when both the therapist and the client would look at the
progress made in Martin's grappling with the problem, a sort of ongoing assessment. It took about a couple of moths for him to come to a decision. He
increased his payment towards board and at the same time arrived at the realisation that he was an autonomous being with responsibility of his own. This was a
movement towards differentiation.

His difficulties with love-relationships remained crucial during the best part of
therapy. His heterosexual relationships had always been ambivalent and confused. On the one hand were his intense sexual needs and the need to love as also
to be loved. On the other was his puritanical attitude towards petting of any
kind. He had always been reluctant to look at the true state of his mind with
regard to this conflict. When he started therapy he had a girl friend who was
depressed and very anxious. On two occasions she had been hospitalised for varying periods for psychiatric treatment. Martin's relationship towards her was one
of mutual dependence. There was heavy petting whenever they met and Martin
would come away unhappy as also guilty. Again he seemed to sustain this relationship just because he believed this was the way the way a "normal" young man
of his age would behave. His relationship to this girl was one of physical attraction without much consideration of her as a person. The physical pleasure he
obtained seemed to be the main motive for the sustenance of his friendship. Martin did not realise this fact but was frankly puzzled at his guilt feelings. The need
here was to increase his awareness of his motivational pattern. This was accomplished by establishing a cognitive and emotional picture of what he thought was
a meaningful love relationship. To start with his expressed ideas were only copies
of his rationalised version of what love meant. By talking about this and explor-
ing concepts his awareness gradually increased. He was helped too with "models"
which the therapist outlined for his consideration. One of the major outcomes
was his willingness to break down the dichotomy of "good love" versus "bad
love." Although he did not express the dichotomy in those terms, at one stage of
his unfolding awareness he labelled his own love as bad because of its emphasis on
sex-oriented pleasure. When he was able to instil some responsibility into the love
relationship, he decided that the only way in which he could evince his responsibility was to discuss the relationship with his girl friend and either produce a
holistic relationship or end the unsatisfactory one. The girl, on her part, was
going through the same difficulty as Martin. They both came to the conclusion

that their sense of responsibility required them to end the relationship, which, while making them both feels guilty did nothing to make it really meaningful. So the relationship was ended. Martin started going out with other girls. He wanted to be spontaneous and not conform to strategies in his love relationships, but he also felt that he should exercise more of responsibility. At the time of writing, Martin had not really established a steady, meaningful relationship with one girl. While it is premature to say whether or not he will be able to do so, Martin does show a progressively evolving awareness of his own role as a man in a love relationship. His psychopathological reactions have decreased.

His striving for restoration of self-esteem has taken the shape of his trying to obtain jobs that could be considered prestigious. His own job as a skilled machinist brought him a very good income but his work-mates were people with very little formal schooling and still less sophistication. Martin looked upon the people around him as having an evaluatory effect on him. While he didn't actually try to keep up with the Joneses, he depended rather heavily on others for elevation of his self-esteem. This aspect was one of the most difficulty to deal with, the method of therapy outlined here being of a holistic nature, the various aspects of Martin's life were not looked at in isolation. His self-esteem being an integral part of his personality gestalt also rose with every therapeutic encounter and with efforts at coping with other problems. The job situation specifically was difficult to resolve as Martin seemed dissatisfied with its nature, not that he couldn't cope with it, but that it was not the kind of thing he would like to carry on as a profession. In this he was perhaps led to model his aspiration on his father who is a successful accountant and therefore qualified as a "white-collar" worker. Martin, after adequate reflection decided that he would take on a clerical job. He went about it with great determination, got the job he wanted and then resigned the old one. Here again he showed responsible decision and action in contrast to his erstwhile impulsivity.

One of Martin's life styles was his dichotomising tendency as result of which he made judgments constantly, most of those dealing with his own behaviour. He seemed rigid in this regard and could never break away from the good or bad aspect of things. He was convinced that what was not good was essentially bad. For instance, he had convinced himself that his frequent masturbation was very wrong and bad. When he had conceptualised his behaviour in these terms he found it increasingly difficult to control this habit. Later he would feel guilty and become miserable. As the habit itself seemed very strong, it seemed reasonable to attempt to change his attitude to it hoping that when he relaxed this dichotomising tendency, he would find it easier to cope with it. The therapeutic attempt to help Martin break his habitual dichotomising tendency again was part of the total reorientation in thinking. The therapist and he looked at a number of models from actual case studies, discussing the adaptiveness or maladaptiveness respectively of various behaviour patterns of the people concerned. The concepts of good and bad were looked at and compared with those of adaptiveness. These were not mere theoretical exercises but were oriented towards Martin's own behaviour patterns. He also read a good book on sex, which objectively dealt with the behaviour of man, without religious or judgemental connotations. Martin was able to feel that his own habit was not an isolated case, that most boys and unmarried young men had that type of behaviour and that he should not think that he was different. At first these remained "flashes" occurring occasionally but later this attitude of acceptance became a habit. With this his masturbatory activity also became less frequent, causing a reduction in guilt. Martin conceptualised this in his own way and was able to say that too much of striving to control one's behaviour not only aroused anxiety but it also defeated its purpose in a paradoxical manner.

It is almost a year now since Martin terminated his visits to see the writer. He still keeps up his contact and sometimes discusses his life patterns. He is steadily going ahead with is self-actualising programme. He has his misery sometimes but his striving is very realistic and he usually knows when to cease striving. He has also learned to set his aspiration at the right level according to his own estimation.

Conclusion

Human behaviour is both implicit and explicit, some of it unobservable and some observable. In any system aimed at the modification of behaviour these two aspects have to be take into account. Again it is difficult to define what is meant by implicit behaviour. Is it the complex of physiological activity that goes on incessantly within the human organism? Or is it more specifically the activity of the autonomic nervous system? And is there something beyond the mere physiological activity which is a deeper dimension of human experience? The rationale of any therapy is a function of how clearly the fundamental aspects of behaviour have been conceptualised. In this book the term therapy has a special connotation. But it does not carry the connotation of "cure" because cure presupposes a standard state of equilibrium to which all human beings have to be reduced. The fundamental thesis is the uniqueness of the individual. Every human being is different from every other and therefore logically there ought to be as many therapeutic variations as there are people. In other words, behaviour modification has to be tailored to suit every person who needs to profit by it.

If the individual man or woman is to be considered a responsible individual, any modification of behaviour cannot come from without but from within. This is because of the self-regulating nature of the human being. Experiences in living result in change of strategies which expand or modify or limit their further acceptance. It is possible to refer to such processes as constituting selective living, in other words acceptance of some experiences and rejection of others. It is understandable that man should want to change his environment, but he cannot possibly do this without some knowledge of what he is about. If the range of his experience can be increased, an individual could then expand his total behaviour, one of the expected outcomes being the avoidance of boredom and the increase in the range of affect. This latter need not necessarily be considered valuable in itself, but seems a necessary concomitant to the greater separation of the poles in any given existential dimension. In other words one of the main difficulties of living arises when a person's experiences cannot be clearly distinguished in terms of their affective connotations. This phenomenon has been seen as the telescoping of the range due to restricted behaviour. To prevent this happening or to break through this limitation once it has occurred, a person appears to have to undergo some experiences that are usually referred to as distressing. But even here some distinctions have to be made. Take grief and suffering for example. There is no need to postulate that these experiences are similar. On the contrary they have to be looked at as differing in their nature. Suffering is differentiated from grief in that it is a painful experience caused by the presence of something noxious or intense, within the organism or outside of it. Grief can then be seen as a reaction to the loss of or absence of an experience seen as essential. The difference between these two experiences is illustrated by the expressions like "the cup of sorrows" being full when referring to suffering and by feelings of emptiness when speaking of grief.

There can be patterns of grief as it progresses from tangible losses to very subtle ones. Congenital conditions like deformities or absence of organs are sources of grief when these are perceived as a lack in the experiencer but present in the people around him. This grief can therefore be seen as caused by a desire towards conformity, that is its aetiology lies in a referential experience. Injuries, which deprive a person of limbs or of sensations over parts of the body, can cause grief because of another type of referential experience, in this case not perhaps with intact human beings around him but with his own existential state prior to the bereavement.

Infants and adults alike share grief and parting from a loved person or at loss of love. Children of a very tender age do not discriminate between a person and the love he gives. They also do not accept the finality of death but continue to expect the loved-object to return. Adult human beings also sometimes deny the finality of death.

It is perhaps not the loss of the attachment itself which causes grief but the failure to have distinguished between 'having' and 'possessing'. If the objects (this includes people) are considered as extensions of one's own self, the grief reaction becomes intense because one is grieving for part of the self perceived as lost. A more autonomous person learns to have love-objects without possessing and incorporating them in his self.

Looked at in another way, the inability to have loved objects without possessing them could be viewed as inadequate sampling. A meaningful life involves both the pleasurable and the painful aspects of existence. If life becomes a pursuit of pleasurable experiences only, one segment of the experiential pattern remains unfilled; this might lead to grief which can then be seen as a reaction to the absence of meaning. Experience to be meaningful perhaps must be associated with a reality situation. This definition of reality is partly based on the functioning of our nervous system which seems to operate by contrasts. Physiological tensions of various kinds (seen as unpleasurable) build up occasionally and when relieved create the perception of pleasure.

Grief can be seen as a reaction occurring in a vacuum because it is to a situation that does not exist any more. On the other hand, suffering can be more meaningful because it is related to the presence of something perceived as a reality, however painful.

The conclusion seems reasonable that grief should be eschewed whenever possible and suffering accepted in its place. This does not mean a denial of grief if it already exists but its conversion into a more meaningful experience. It is possible to accomplish this by experiencing the pain as a present characteristic of the experiencing self, not as absence of the loved object. The emphasis of the experience is withdrawn from the object and transferred to the subject. This shift in emphasis is a conversion of the emptiness of grief into the pain of existential suffering.

In reaction to loss of love-objects two extremes are usually seen. A person feels grief but because the norms of most cultures require him to be brave, he may divert his attention to other matters. This is maladaptive because the problem of grief has not been coped with, but only shelved for the time being. At the other extreme, a person who goes into prolonged mourning confirms the decimation of his self. Both methods distort existential realities, the first by turning away from the self and the second by distorting the meaning of an experience. Feelings of emptiness may be expected to result. Grieving avoids the full impact of the pain, which, if experienced, would be suffering. This can also be looked at as an unwillingness to tolerate greater awareness of the self and existential realities. Authenticity and continual self-actualisation cannot be attained except by intense striving. It is perhaps not accidental that large number of human beings elects a "minimal-effort" life instead.

Despite its ubiquity, grief is not reality oriented. To increase one's awareness of the self and of reality one has to be able to undergo suffering rather than grief. It can therefore be hypothesised that it would be extremely difficult for a human being not to have the experience of suffering and still have expectation of nobler states of being.

The therapeutic system adumbrated in this book is geared towards a fuller experiencing of affective states when they do occur. Therapeutic intervention itself has been seen as a deliberate exercise in doing just that. It is hoped that with the extension of the range of experience will also come the ability to distinguish more clearly amongst affective states. These experiences in turn are expected to cause an increase in awareness.

SECTION TWO
—
GALLIMAUFRY

East and west, will the twain ever meet?

Australia can now be said to be at the socio-cultural crossroads in as much as the experiment in multicultural living, integrating diverse cultures into a meaningful whole, is well under way. Not only does this massive undertaking involve very many European cultures, but it also includes cultures from Asia, Africa and Latin America. Two important approaches are discernible in the official circles. The first and most direct method is the attempt to *assimilate* the long-term visitor, in other words to make his/her behaviour patterns to approximate to the general concept of an Australian culture. The second, which can be seen as a bewildered approach, is the attempt to understand the culture of the newly arrived people from overseas. Both these do not seem to be very effective as they are mainly aimed at creating a "homogeneous" culture. A certain unwillingness to look at and to understand the essential differences is a fundamental aspect of Australian attempts to create a super-integrated society. Well meaning people have set up systems of international living, of local hosting and so on without having touched even the fringe areas of the cultural situation.

This paper therefore is an attempt to compare two different types of culture, which are essentially and utterly diverse. For the sake of economy of conceptualisation and convenience I shall refer to these cultures as those of the East and of the West. To be specific I have chosen the Indian culture as representing the East because I am familiar with it. By Western culture I mean specifically the British and the Australian for the same reason of familiarity. I hasten to add that my statements here should not be construed as incontrovertible facts but only as a workable hypothesis for the purpose of study

The crux of the matter lies within the concepts of reality and normality in the East and the West. In the West the tangible outer world is the real one. Therefore the normal person in that culture is the extraverted one with outgoing interests. India, with its insistence on the inner world of the intangible as the reality, considers the introvert with his inward-directed gaze as representing normality. In conformity with these concepts it is easy to see that deviance from normality in each culture brings the person concerned closer to being "normal" in the other culture.

And stemming from habits of looking within or without arise the doctrine of Negation and Affirmation respectively. In India, for instance, the concept of Maya dismisses many of the tangible manifestations of phenomenon as being illusory or of being less important. The Indian search for truth and reality leads a member of that culture to discard or negate the tangible by saying: "This is not it." The man from the Western world affirms and labels all observable phenomena. Therefore his doctrine is one of Affirmation. A fanciful analogy would perhaps make the meaning clear. Imagine an Indian and a Westerner poised at different points on the periphery of a forest about to start on a quest to discover a treasure buried somewhere in the middle of the forest. Assume also that both have maps with the position of the treasure clearly marked. The Indian, with his dismissal of what he considers unreal, pays scant attention to the flora and fauna however attractive these might be. He tries to reach the treasure by the most direct route without letting himself be distracted by other phenomena. The Westerner appreciates the attractive objects and feels impelled to label the beautiful trees, flowers and animals. He has to know more about them. His quest eventually leads him to the treasure but only after he has savoured all the tangible manifestations.

Societies, which emphasise the tangible as being important, consider individual man as the hub of the Universe. His movement in the existential dimension is thought to be centrifugal, from the centre to the periphery. Consequently, social systems are geared to his maximal physical comfort and enjoyment.

The human race as a whole rather than individual life is of more consequence to the Indian. Man stands at the periphery of the Cosmos in company with innumerable other human beings. His movement is centripetal from the periphery to the core of cosmic consciousness.

Stemming from the tendency to centrifugal and centripetal movements respectively, there are two concepts regarding the significance of all life. In Western societies, which consider individual life as being important, and which therefore emphasise the doctrine of affirmation, individual life is of the utmost value. They seek to preserve health and comforts and to prolong life as much as possible.

Societies which have the existential movement in a centripetal direction do not emphasise the **value** of individual life, but they pay great attention to **reverence** for life leading to concepts of Ahimsa and detachment. Thus in Indian philosophy non-killing is a consequence of reverence for life. The legalised killing sanctioned in the West–of animals and men–is aimed at the preservation of individual life and is seen to emphasise the value of human life.

The cultural differences of the east and West carry over to concepts of religion, music and thinking. Centrifugal civilisations of the West easily accept vicarious experience as valid, as for instance one man dying for another and saving the second from damnation. They also accept a limited human existence during which every man is judged according to his goodness. Once having accepted a limitation to human existence, it stands to reason that man's physical comforts should be catered to in the best possible manner.

In centripetal cultures with their emphasis on reverence for life rather than on the value of life, the individual is considered the master of his destiny. He breaks the causal link of Karma only by his individualistic efforts. No one else can suffer for him or expiate his sins. This means that man must accept full responsibility for his behaviour.

The Western concepts of living in closely knit communities with a great deal of physical proximity made available at work and at pleasure, result in communal togetherness. In other words individual differences are sought to be obliterated in a composite social manifestation. In conformity with this characteristic, Western musical forms have developed compositions which make use of harmony amongst sounds. Eastern societies despite their densities tolerate much more individuality amongst its members in that there is little of the levelling influence which makes for conformity in the West. The result is the creation of greater autonomy and liberty for the individual to develop in his own special way. Even when many instruments or voices are made use of in a musical performance in India, only the melody is manifest. It is easy to see the connection between this and the doctrine of Negation, which encourages single-mindedness in apprehending reality.

The thinking pattern of the East and the West also differ. People of the East are Divergent thinkers working from the concrete to the abstract. Their Gestalt thinking can be likened to the ever-widening ripples caused on the surface of a still pond when a stone falls into it. Western thinking is Convergent in that it consists in the processing of a mass of data leading to specific, limited conclusions. Consonant with this type of thinking is the avoidance of generalisations in the absence of adequate data. In other words Western thinking emphasises objectivity. The Eastern thinking, because of its Gestalt nature, emphasises complementarity.

Extraverted and introverted cultures differ in another important respect as well. The former, which emphasises the reality of the tangible, must make life as pleasant as possible for its members. Individuals are therefore encouraged to seek experiences that are pleasurable and to avoid those that cause distress even in a small measure. In other words only one aspect of existence is savoured. It is wrong to presume that the Indian culture enjoins its members to pursue suffering for its own sake. What it really tries to teach is the need to savour all aspects of existence and not to avoid suffering if it becomes inevitable. To sum all this up, the Western culture is prepared to tolerate lowered awareness of existence if it means eradication of suffering. The Eastern culture opts for maximal awareness of the self and of reality even at the risk of exposing its members to experiences of suffering in the process.

I am sure that enough has been said to make it clear that the Western and Eastern cultures are dissimilar. And yet people are striving to merge these into a meaningful system. Their attempts at integration have failed so far because of two important reasons. First and foremost, the people of the West have not really attempted a synthesis of cultures. They have tried assimilation, which really means the persuasion of the Indian to accept the Western culture. Secondly, the West has consistently refused to accept that differences in culture, as the ones delineated above, do exist. So all attempts at the development of a homogeneous culture represent attempts at incorporation. Glib proponents of a doctrine of acculturation believe it is possible to delete or modify some aspects of these cultures to accomplish a miraculous integration. This cannot be done except by the destruction of one or the other way of life. This paper therefore pleads for tolerance of diversity, of cultures co-existing with each trying to understand the other without attempting incorporation. Acceptance of such a pattern of co-existence would reduce speculation as to which is the better civilisation and perhaps reduce prejudices which are now being maintained by one culture having to adopt patterns from the other.

It has to be granted that in India for instance there is a tendency to adopt the external trappings of the West such as clothing and culinary preparations. Many recent visitors to India have reported on this phenomenon especially among young people. But I consider these sorties as being only peripheral. The real question however, is this; will the East and West ever meet in a meaningful way? I leave it to the reader to answer this in the best way he or she can!

Synchronicity

Carl Jung, responsible for originating the idea of the Collective Unconscious, had always been interested in phenomena like extrasensory perception, telepathy, and clairvoyance, for which conventional science has provided no adequate explanation, nor has it developed the appropriate tools of enquiry. He gave an explanation, which supplements causality, naming it Synchronicity which he defined as "a coincidence in time, of two or more causally unrelated events, which have the same or similar meaning." In other words the structure of reality includes a principle of acausal connection, which manifests itself most conspicuously in the form of meaningful coincidences. This could take the form of a coincidence of inner perceptions such as foreboding, dreams, visions and the like, with outward events located in the past, or the present, or the future. It can be said that coincidence is at the core of the concept of Synchronicity. The mathematician Warren Weaver gives an excellent example of this kind of coincidence. This happened in Nebraska, USA. In one of the local churches, the choir practice was scheduled for 7.20 p.m. on the 1st of March 1950. All the fifteen members of the choir belonging to ten families were late. The minister's wife was delayed because she was ironing her daughter's dress. Another girl was delayed because she had to finish her geometry lesson. Yet another girl wanted to listen to an interesting radio programme. For another member, her car would not start. Every one of those ten families had a mundane reason for not being able to go to Church at the scheduled time. It was just as well. At 7.30 p.m. a fierce explosion destroyed the church. All the fifteen members of the choir were saved because they were delayed due to various reasons. Some of them wondered whether their miraculous escape was due to an 'Act of God.'

There is another type of synchronicity in which a meaningful precognition seems to be involved. Consider this story by Edgar Allan Poe in which three shipwrecked sailors in an open boat killed and ate the fourth, a cabin boy whose name was Richard Parker. Several years later three shipwreck survivors in an open boat killed and ate the cabin boy whose name was, strangely, Richard Parker. At the trial of the three men in 1884 the coincidence with the Poe story was duly brought out. The Cabin Boy Cannibalism case seems to be a meaningful coincidence, a chance coincidence and a precognitive inspiration by Edgar Allan Poe.

Alan Vaughan, a leading authority on synchronicity, speaks about the Synchronicity of Synchronicity by which he means that his thinking or writing about this subject tends to produce actual synchronicity. In 1971 Alan, after giving a talk on synchronicity in Chicago, was waiting for a plane back to New York. When his plane was announced he happened to glance over the shoulder of a woman who was reading an article about him. He reached over her shoulder and pointed out an error in the article. She was startled as she recognized him from the picture in the article. Alan explained that this was not chance coincidence but synchronicity triggered by talking about synchronicity.

Sometimes a chance encounter can be so incredible as to boggle the imagination. Dr. Warren Weaver in his book "Lady luck: The theory of probability" describes one such case. A Mr. George D. Bryson was making a business trip from St. Louis to New York. At Louisville he had a stopover. He enquired at the station for the leading hotel, which was the Brown Hotel where he registered. Just for fun he asked the mail clerk if there was any mail for him. The clerk handed him a letter addressed to Mr. George D.Bryson, Room 307, that being the number of the room to which he had just been assigned. It turned out that the preceding resident of Room 307 was another George D. Bryson! Eventually the two Brysons met and had a hearty laugh at this incredible coincidence. Alan Vaughan describes this as a Chance Encounter of the First Kind.

Another case cited by Jung has been described as a Chance Encounter of the Second Kind. Shortly before the outbreak of World War 1, a German lady took a photograph of her small son and left the film plate to be developed in Strasbourg. But the beginning of the war made it impossible for her to collect it. Two years later, she bought another film to photograph her baby daughter. When the film was developed it was a double exposure. The picture underneath was that of her small son taken before the outbreak of the War. Did she imprint a thought-photograph of her first child onto the picture of her second?

Jung quotes a case in his book Synchronicity about a M. Deschamps, when a boy in Orleans, was once given a piece of plum pudding by a M.de Fortgibu. Ten years later he encountered another plum pudding in a Paris restaurant. When he asked whether he could have a piece, it turned out that M.de Fortgibu had already ordered the pudding. Many years later M.Deschamps was invited to partake of a plum pudding also in Paris. While he was eating it he remarked that the only thing lacking was M.de Fortgibu. Who should walk in then but an old man in the last stages of disorientation! It was M.de Fortgibu who had burst in on the party by mistake.

Incredible coincidences very often happen with things instead of people. Alan Vaughan was working his way through college and he had a part time job at the Akron Public Library in the order department. The wages were low but there was the fringe benefit of ordering books and records at a discount. The RCA Company was bringing out the first complete recording of the nine Beethoven symphonies by Toscanini. The album was sumptuously bound and contained a removable metal medallion bearing the likeness of Toscanini. But the price of $50 was far beyond his budget. A friend wanted the album and he asked Alan to order it for him. When the package arrived from the dealer in New York there were two albums but the bill was only for one. So Alan got what he wanted free.

The famous anthropologist Professor Elkin who has done extensive work with the Aboriginal people of Australia gives an account of synchronicity, which is nothing short of mysterious. Once he was invited to attend two meetings of Aboriginal elders about 100 miles apart, taking place at the same time. He attended one of them. During the meeting he was not sure which of the meetings he was at. Not only that, he seemed to be aware of the things discussed at both meetings. This is synchronicity at its very best.

The Yogis of India have long been aware of the phenomenon of a person becoming aware of music of inconceivable beauty that seems to emanate from no apparent source. Sometimes this sound known in Sanskrit as NADA is referred to as the Music of the Spheres. In this connection it is good to go back to the experiment of Dr. Wilder Penfield, Director of the Montreal Neurological Institute, who showed that by stimulating the temporal lobe of the brain, a subject will "hear" music. One of Penfield's subjects was sure that someone had turned on a radio or a record player. So realistic was the music that he heard! Many instances have been reported in the Psychic Research magazines. Dr. Alan Vaughan wanted to write on this subject when he found he had only one case on hand. He was amazed when a young woman in Washington sent him a detailed account of three cases of NADA.

Those of us who are interested in the therapeutic uses of hypnosis would be aware that sometimes clients in a deep state say that they have travelled out of their bodies and have visited friends or relatives. On awakening from the hypnotic state they are usually able describe very accurately the environments they have thus visited. Uri Geller, noted for his prowess at bending spoons with the power of the mind, recounts a remarkable thing that happened to him. He was visiting his friend Andrija Puharich, a well-known psychic researcher, and he fell fast asleep on his friend's couch. Geller found himself projected out of his body. His astral body was standing on a street corner in Rio de Janeiro. Someone rushed up and put a 1000-cruzeiro note in his hand. When Geller later came back into his body and woke up, he opened his hand to show his friend the 1000-Cruzeiro note!

One of the implications of the concept of synchronicity is the seamlessness of the universe. This ties in with the Vedantic formulations, which Hindus espouse. Jung claims to have found evidence for the interconnectedness of everything in the Universe in his study of I Ching, a method of Chinese divination. He says of this method: "While the Western mind carefully sifts, weighs, selects, classifies and isolates, the Chinese picture of the moment encompasses everything down to the minutest nonsensical detail, because all of the ingredients make up the observed moment."

Peter A. Jordan, who writes extensively on Jungian philosophy, sums up the entire aspect of synchronicity in these words: "So, if the modern alliance among quantum physicists, neuroscientists, parapsychologists and mystics is not just a short-fused phase in scientific understanding, a paradigm shift may well be imminent. We may soon not only embrace a new image of the Universe as non-causal and sympathetic, but uncover conclusive evidence that the universe functions not as some great machine, but as a great thought—unifying matter, energy and consciousness....... At that point, our perceptions and hence our world, will be changed forever." An apt paraphrase of Vedanta philosophy! It may be satisfying for us, who cherish our Indian heritage, to know that at last the West is coming to our way of thinking.

The Dynamics Of Terrorism

In recent times there has been a great deal of confusion in defining the term "terrorist". The most popular impression is that anyone who has been implicated in violence, especially if that violence results in the injury or the killing, of large numbers of people, stands condemned as a "terrorist". Some people who imagine they are more discriminating, like to make a distinction between "freedom fighters" and "terrorists." The problem of definition is further complicated by the fact that many people who, for one reason or the other, commit violent acts to further the cause of minority groups, are first dubbed terrorists, but later on when they have succeeded in what they had wished to achieve, have been renamed freedom fighters. One of the classic examples of this has been Nelson Mandela. Although at one stage of his life he advocated violence as a legitimate tool in the abolition of apartheid, after he became the President of South Africa, he developed into a seasoned diplomat, in every respect the embodiment of tolerance. In India, during the fight for freedom from British rule, Sri Aurobindo, an educator, was said to have been a terrorist. He was arrested, tried and imprisoned. It was while he was in prison he decided to abjure violence and turn to Yoga, becoming one of the greatest thinkers of the world.

Many people believe that those who perform acts of terror are abnormal in some way. Nothing can be further from the truth. It is very hard to find one who is mentally ill or who suffers from some kind of psychological deviance like the psychoses. That is why when later a person has been identified as having committed some terrorist act his erstwhile neighbours find it hard to comprehend that he could do such a thing. The fifteen-year-old American boy who flew his plane into the American Express Building is an instance in point. The majority of so-called terrorists are ordinary people who cannot be picked out from the population at large. However many of them seem to be idealists with a compelling mission in life, namely to redress the wrongs suffered by a group of people or a nation. Contrary to popular opinion these people seem to lead exemplary clean lives avoiding the manifold sins afflicting the modern world. Many of them give up a life of ease and comfort for the "Cause." They have very often a firm belief in God and that He would look after them. Further they believe in a world to come after this life,

95

which is more beautiful and meaningful than the present one. This makes them fearless of death and dying.

Unless the West addresses the causes for terrorism, this menace will always be with us. The causes are easy to identify although those responsible are oblivious to them. Among these are:

- The philosophy of the superpowers that might is always right.

- The compelling need for them to play God.

- The patent lack of any semblance of justice they bring to bear on the problems of the world.

- Their constant interference in the internal affairs of other countries.

- The use of their immense wealth and military power to prop up puppet governments and dictators of their choice.

- Their use of the secret service to implement their nefarious activities.

- Their use of the so-called third world countries to test weapons of mass destruction. This has happened in Iraq and Afghanistan quite recently.

- The waste of billions of dollars in wars whereas this money could have been used for the amelioration of misery in the world.

- Their switch of allegiances to suit their needs and convenience.

- The use of money aid and food as tools of persuasion to force their own philosophies and way of life on other nations.

- Disregard for the culture of other nations.

- Disregard for the tenets of the United Nations.

- Disregard for justice and humaneness when dealing with nations especially non-European ones.

To sum it all up, they have walked roughshod over the nations of the world. When one considers all the above, it is easy to see why terrorist organisations spring up all over the world to redress the wrongs that have been perpetrated on the peoples of the world. This is not to say that anyone can condone the terrible things that happened on the 11th of September 2001 resulting in the loss of thousands of innocent lives. There is no justification for that carnage. But from the point of view of the terrorists, perhaps they believe that the end justifies the means.

The West lost a good opportunity during the post 11th September days, to come to grips with the problem and to eradicate the causes of terrorism. Instead of rushing into war and devastating a whole country, the Western Nations could have helped the needy of the world. They could have listened to rational voices and could have even negotiated with terrorist groups. It is important to remember that at least one superpower was responsible for encouraging and fostering terrorist cells in many countries. So negotiating with the same terrorists does not seem such a dreadful thing after all. By going to war, the superpowers have made matters worse. The terrorists have only gone underground and can rise up at any time. The world will never again be a safe place.

Going to war goes against commonsense. Social scientists will tell you that punishment never reforms the wrongdoer but only makes him more stubborn. Rewards, on the contrary, will work wonders. What the Western countries ranged against terrorism are doing, is to wreak vengeance. Their bombs have killed hundreds of innocent people including women and children in the present war but they do make no apologies for it. When they put their captives in cages and shackle them saying that these are not prisoners of war, we can see their irrational hatred.

Arundhati Roy of Literary fame, writing in The Guardian, has this to say; "Here is a list of the countries that America has been at war with–and bombed– since the Second World War. China (1945-46, 1950-53), Korea (1950-53), Guatemala (1954, 1967-69), Indonesia (1958), Cuba (1959-60), the Belgian Congo (1964), Peru (1965), Laos (1964-73), Cambodia (1969-70), Grenada (1983), Libya (1986), El Salvador (1980s), Nicaragua (1980), Panama (1989), Iraq (1991-99), Bosnia (1995), Yugoslavia (1999) And now Afghanistan and Iraq.

Certainly it does not tire–this, the most free nation in the world.

What freedoms does it uphold? Within its borders, the freedoms of speech, religion, thought, of artistic expression, food habits, sexual preferences and many other exemplary, wonderful things. Outside its borders, the freedom to dominate, humiliate and subjugate–usually in the service of America's real religion, the 'free market.' So, when the US Government christens a war 'Operation Infinite Justice' or 'Operation Enduring Freedom' we in the third world feel more than a tremor of fear. Because we know that Infinite Justice for some means Infinite Injustice for others. And Enduring Freedom for some means Enduring Subjugation for others.

The International Coalition Against Terror is a cabal of the richest countries in the world. Between them, they manufacture and sell almost all of the world's weapons; they possess the largest stockpile of weapons of mass destruction–chemical, biological and nuclear. They have fought the most wars, account for most of the genocide, subjection, ethnic cleansing and human rights violations in modern history, and have sponsored, armed and financed untold numbers of dictators and despots. Between them they have worshipped, almost deified, the cult of violence and war."

Even now it is not too late to make amends. Reasonable people all over the world will ask those who are making war, to stop now and build up the countries they have helped to destroy. If as the Western Nations are always saying that they are Christians, they have to consider the Biblical injunction of God: "Vengeance is mine". No human being can arrogate to himself the right to wreak vengeance for whatever reason.

It is also important to remember that the immortal prayer of the dying Christ, "Father forgive them, for they know not what they do" applies both to the so-called terrorists and to those who wage war against them.

The Worst Act of Terrorism in History

It all began with a prayer. Before Colonel Paul W. Tibbets of the United States Army Air force took off in his B-29 bomber named **Enola Gay** on his dastardly mission on the 6th of August 1945, the chaplain William Downey recited a special prayer for the success of the mission. He prayed that God would protect the aircrew and that "armed with Thy might they may bring this war to a rapid end." The Chaplin knew that the taking of human life under any circumstances was forbidden by Christian doctrine; perhaps he believed that Americans had a special dispensation from God to do as they liked on this earth! (The same thing has happened recently in Afghanistan and Iraq. It is worth mentioning that President Bush and Prime Minister Blair both prayed in their respective churches for victory in their unjust war.) The unchristian aspect of this prayer is that it made no mention of the victims, women, children and men who were to die a horrible death. The mission then was to drop an atom bomb, more destructive than anything seen before, on the Japanese city of Hiroshima. At 8.14 a.m. on that fateful day, Tibbets ordered his crew to put on Polaroid goggles to protect their eyes. Soon after, the B-29 had arrived over its aiming point the Aioi Bridge in the centre of Hiroshima.

At that time in the history of the World War 2, Hiroshima had not been heavily bombed. There was very little air defence over the city because the Japanese Air Force had been decimated. On that summer morning the streets were filled with people walking and cycling to work. The first flash of the explosion was as bright as a thousand suns. Those nearest the epicentre of the explosion were vaporised or burned to a cinder. Those further away had their hair and skin burned off. Many were blinded. The blast that followed the flash caused untold destruction of houses and factories. Violent winds whipped up firestorms. Thousands of people jumped into the river and were drowned. The Hiroshima Government has estimated that 140,000 people were killed outright and an area of the city within a radius of 10 kilometres was completely devastated. Many more people died within a month as a result of exposure to gamma radiation. General

Dwight D. Eisenhower who was the Supreme Commander of the Allied Forces in Europe in 1945 and a future President of the USA was against the use of the atom bomb. He later described his reactions thus:-"I was getting more and more depressed just thinking about it. Then he (Truman) asked for my opinion, so I told him I was against it on two counts. First, the Japanese were ready to surrender and it wasn't necessary to hit them with that awful thing. Second, I hated to see our country be the first to use such a weapon." Truman and other US leaders always said that they had had to choose between using the bomb and invading Japan at the cost of many American lives. There were other alternatives though. They could have defeated Japan by a sea blockade and by conventional bombardment. Or they could have waited for a little while till the Soviet attack on Japan would end the war. In the final analysis it has to be said that Truman and others really wanted to test the destructive potential of the atom bomb. Three days after the bombing of Hiroshima, another B-29 carrying a Plutonium bomb called 'Fat Man" took off on a second bombing mission. Although it was destined for the city of Kokura, atrocious weather conditions over the city had reduced visibility considerably. So Major Charles W. Sweeny, who commanded the B-29, dropped the bomb on Nagasaki Port. The Peace Memorial Park in Nagasaki has recorded the following statistics about the devastation the bomb caused.

Dead: 73,884
Injured: 74,909
Sufferers: 120,820
Houses burned down: 11,574
Houses half-ruined: 5509
Houses partly damaged: 50,000

The devastation of Hiroshima and Nagasaki was due to three main types of effects, the blast, thermal radiation and nuclear radiation. The blast effect of an atomic device is similar to that of a conventional explosive but much more intense and far-reaching. Thermal radiation, which results from the extremely high temperatures created by an atomic explosion causes serious burns on exposed parts of the body and would ignite fires over a large area. Nuclear radiation, which results from the neutrons and gamma rays associated with fission, causes death and injury as a result of damage to living tissue. Unprotected persons up to a distance of about a mile from a point directly below the explosion were affected. The survivors of the attacks on Hiroshima and Nagasaki, known as **hibakusha** suffered intensely all through their lives.

Two more atomic bombs were ready to be dropped on cities of Japan, perhaps on Tokyo, but mercifully further cruelty was not to be. The British philosopher Bertrand Russell, who became an activist against nuclear arms, had this to say about the state of the world: "I think the existence of the Hydrogen bomb presents a perfectly clear alternative to all the governments of the world. Will they submit to an international authority, or shall the human race die out?"

It was in the year 1939 when the Second World War began that scientists in the USA and some other Western countries first realised the possibility of building an atomic bomb. Albert Einstein had brought to the notice of the authorities the possibility of splitting of the atom and causing a chain reaction to release enormous amounts of energy. Although scientists were feverishly working on this idea no one really knew how long it would take to build that bomb. It is of interest to note that President Franklin D. Roosevelt of the USA was initially against the use of such a weapon even if the American scientists succeeded in producing it. He said: "The ruthless bombing from the air of civilians during the past few years which has resulted in the maiming and in the death of thousands of defenceless men, women and children has profoundly shocked the conscience of humanity." Had he lived long enough, perhaps the atomic bomb might not have been used on the civilian population of Hiroshima. Harry Truman who succeeded Roosevelt had no such qualms about murdering innocent civilians.

The Manhattan Project under the command of Brigadier-General Leslie R. Groves with Robert Oppenheimer as scientific director had a team of top scientists working on producing the atomic bomb first, before the Germans could succeed. It is also significant to note that many of the scientists involved in the project were Jewish refugees from Germany. In Los Alamos which was the primary site of this research, there was unprecedented security and restrictions on the personnel. This and the total secrecy under which everything was done, caused a great deal of hardship to the scientists and to their families. Although Japan and Germany had the capability to produce the bomb they did not put enough resources behind the task. In the USA however, the President gave the Manhattan Project limitless money, hiding the secret spending from the Congress and the public. It has been estimated that two billion dollars were spent in producing the atom bomb. By the end of 1944, General Groves was able to tell the President of the USA that the bomb would be ready in the summer of 1945. It is an estimate of the callousness of the people who were instrumental in producing this fearsome instrument of war that they felt that if the enemy were defeated before the bomb was ready it would be an effort wasted!

Japan was close to surrender in July 1945, which fact was known to the Allied leaders but not to the American and British people. They knew from intercepted messages that Japan had sent to its ambassadors abroad, that many leaders in Japan including Emperor Hirohito backed those in favour of peace. The Japanese had by then realised that their position was hopeless. The Emperor even planned to send a former Prime Minister, Prince Konoye to Moscow to try to negotiate a peace deal. On the 16th of July 1945 President Truman met Winston Churchill, the British Prime Minister and Joseph Stalin, the Soviet dictator at Potsdam on the outskirts of Berlin. They issued the Potsdam Declaration, which called for the unconditional surrender of all Japanese armed forces. The alternative for Japan was prompt and utter destruction. It made no mention of the atom bomb. The wily Western leaders were thirsting for revenge for the Japanese attack on Pearl Harbour on 7th December 1941 in Hawaii in which 3500 US servicemen were killed and 4 American battleships sunk. The following day the USA and Britain had declared war on Japan.

The recent cruelty of the Americans, the British and the Australians too, in their attacks on Afghanistan and Iraq comes as no wonder. Their use of depleted uranium shells and cluster bombs proves this. Guantanamo Bay will no doubt haunt them till the end of their days as also the inhuman treatment the Americans have inflicted on the so-called terrorists. They are inured against the killing of innocent men, women and children. They have always done it in the past and will do so in the future. We must not forget that the USA has the largest collection of Weapons of Mass Destruction, enough to destroy all life on earth many times over. They seem to be above the law. No inspectors haunt their caches of weapons! In the meanwhile, all of us have to cower with bated breath beneath the shadow of the looming mushroom cloud!

Tales Of Love And Gallantry

Savitri And Satyavan

I do hope, most Indian children know the beautiful story of Satyavan and Savitri. She was a princess and he was the son of a deposed King. Satyavan lived as a hermit in the forest with his parents. In one of Savitri's journeys in her chariot, she came across Satyavan who was walking in the forest. She fell in love with him and resolved to marry him. There was one hitch though. The sage Narada who happened to be on a visit to the court of King Asvapati (Savitri's father) knew that Satyavan was doomed to die within a year. However Savitri would not be dissuaded from her resolve. So the devoted couple was married, and Savitri went to the forest to live with her husband. The year passed blissfully. Meanwhile Satyavan had no inkling that his days on earth were coming to an end. On the fateful day, Savitri insisted on accompanying her husband on his usual hunting expedition. While they were in the heart of the forest, Satyavan felt faint and fell to the ground. Savitri tended to him but he soon became still. Then she saw Yama the God of Death coming towards Satyavan. Yama slipped a noose around Satyavan and carried him away. But Savitri was determined to follow the God of Death. After a time, Yama heard her footsteps and looked back. He asked her not to follow him but to go back to the land of the living. But she would not be dissuaded. She said to Yama that the scriptures say that walking seven steps together with another person makes him a friend. She had walked more than seven steps with the God of Death. Yama was pleased with her answer and said he would grant her any boon except her husband's life. She asked him to restore the sight to her father-in-law and also his kingdom. This was granted. But still Savitri followed him. Yama turned back and said to her that she should make arrangements for the funeral of Satyavan's body and that she should desist from following him, whereupon Savitri remarked that without the soul the body was no good. So Yama granted her more boons. Savitri thereupon asked that she have one hundred sons. Without realising what he was saying, Yama granted her that boon too. Still she followed him. When Yama looked back again, she asked how this boon could work seeing that she had lost her husband. Yama knew that he could not go back on his word. So he restored Satyavan's life.

Orpheus And Eurydice

No love story is more poignant than that of Orpheus and his wife Eurydice. Orpheus was an excellent musician and a player on the lyre. His music was so sweet that it used to put to sleep the most fearsome of monsters. He accompanied the Argonauts to Colchis in their quest for the Golden Fleece. His enchanted playing put to sleep the dragon-serpent guard and in many other ways helped them overcome difficulties. On his return, he married the comely Eurydice. One day, in the valley of the river Peneius, while trying to flee from the attentions of Aristaeus who tried to force his attentions on her, Eurydice trod on a serpent and died of its bite. The disconsolate Orpheus wandered the earth not knowing what to do. Finally he descended into Tartarus the realm of the dead, hoping to fetch her back. With his plaintive music, he charmed the three-headed Dog Cerberus, and the three Judges of the Dead. He also won over the savage heart of Hades who promised to restore Eurydice to the upper world on one condition, that Orpheus should not look behind him until his wife was safely back under the light of the sun. But alas, just before Eurydice was out of the Underworld, her husband looked back to make sure his wife was following, thus breaking the condition of her release. So she had to go back again and all the soothing music Orpheus could play could not bring her back to him.

Psyche And Eros

Psyche was the third daughter of a King. A legend had it that she was born when a dewdrop fell from the sky on the land. She was beautiful, charming and very like a goddess, so much so that a cult grew around her and people began to say that she was the new Aphrodite. But of course, when Aphrodite came to know of it, her indignation knew no bounds. She decided to get rid of her rival. To this end she enlisted the help of her son Eros, the god of love. He is also known as Amor and Cupid.

In the meanwhile, the two older sisters of Psyche got married to kings in the neighbouring countries. The King, her father got worried when no one asked for Psyche's hand in marriage although everyone almost worshipped her. As was the custom in those days in Greece, the King consulted an oracle and was told that Psyche was to be married to Death, the ugliest and most horrible creature that anyone could think of. She was to be taken to the top of a mountain and chained to a rock to be ravished by Death. The King did not realise that Aphrodite was the one who had influenced the oracle to deliver this message. Not content with this, Aphrodite instructed her son Eros to shoot his arrow at Psyche so that she would fall in love with the loathsome beast who would come to claim her. Eros obediently set out to carry out his mother's bidding. Just as he was about to unloose his arrow, he accidentally pricked his finger on it and fell in love with Psyche. Thereupon, he unchained her and got the West Wind to carry her into the Valley of Paradise. Psyche had everything that she could desire. Every night her God-husband Eros visited her. The only conditions he laid on her was that she would not look at him and that she would not inquire into any of his ways. Psyche acquiesced gladly although she did not know what he looked like. She only knew he was loving and kind to her.

It is not clear how the news of Psyche's good fortune reached the ears of her two sisters. They came to the top of the mountain where their sister was once chained and looked down into the Valley of Paradise. They spoke to their sister and got to know everything about her life. That night Psyche told her husband about this. He warned her that disaster would befall her if she paid attention to what her sisters were saying. If Psyche continued to be obedient to him, the child that would be born to her would be a God but if she broke her vow of not questioning, the child would be born a mortal and a girl. Moreover, he Eros would leave her. Eventually Psyche got her husband to agree to her sisters to visit her. Again, they were wafted down by the West Wind into the valley. On their third visit they told Psyche that her husband was actually a serpent, a loathsome creature and that when her baby was born he would devour her and the child. To avert this catastrophe, the sisters told her to keep a lamp in the bedchamber and cover it up. She was also to keep a sharp knife with her. In the middle of the night she should sever the head of her husband. After Eros was asleep, Psyche uncovered the lamp and was amazed to find that her husband was really the god of love and the most good looking person she had ever seen. She felt tremendously guilty and wanted to kill herself with the knife. She fumbled with it and dropped it. While doing all this she accidentally pricked herself on one of her husband's arrows and fell in love with him. A drop of the oil from the lamp fell on her husband's right shoulder and he woke up in pain. Although poor Psyche clung to him in desperation, he accused her of going back on her promise and flew away to his mother.

Psyche suffered intensely and prayed to the many goddesses who would not help her for fear of Aphrodite. Finally she went to Aphrodite herself who put her down in no uncertain terms. She set four tasks for Psyche to do. The first was to sort out the seeds from a huge pile of seeds of many kinds before nightfall, the penalty for failure being death. An army of ants, presumably sent by Eros, accomplished this task before dusk.

The second task was to get some of the Golden Fleece from the ferocious sun rams in a field across the river, again on pain of death. The reeds at the edge of the river advised her to go back at dusk and collect the wool that had been brushed off by the brambles and low hanging boughs of a grove of trees under which the rams often passed. She did exactly this and was able to gather enough of the Golden Fleece to satisfy Aphrodite. In the third test Psyche was given a crystal goblet to obtain water from the Styx, a river that had its source in the depths of hell. That stream was guarded by monsters of all kinds that it was impossible for anyone to get near it. By then Zeus himself was sympathetic to Psyche and to his son Eros, that he sent an eagle to help her. The eagle flew to the centre of the stream and filled the goblet with the water of Styx.

In the final test, Psyche had to go into the underworld and obtain from the hand of Persephone (the Goddess of the dead) a little cask of her own beauty ointment. This time a tower gave her instructions for her journey. Psyche was to take two coins in her mouth and two pieces of barley bread in her hands. She had to refuse to assist a lame donkey driver who would ask her to pick up some sticks. One of the coins was to pay the ferryman over the river Styx. She had to refuse the hand of a dying man reaching up out of the water. Likewise, she had to refuse to help three women weaving the threads of fate. When she came across the three-headed dog Cerberus, she was to throw one of the barley loaves to him. When the three heads started quarrelling over the bread, she was to slip in stealthily. On the way back she should repeat the whole process in reverse. Obeying all these behests, Psyche brought the precious cask of beauty ointment up to the surface of the earth. But she was overwhelmed by the desire to open the casket and use the ointment on her own person. When she opened the casket, only a deadly sleep came out of it and poured over Psyche who fell down as if dead. Eros sensed the danger to his beloved, wiped the sleep off her and put it back in the casket. He took Psyche to Olympus where his father Zeus made her into a goddess. Even Aphrodite was satisfied. Psyche gave birth to a girl, whom the loving couple named as Pleasure.

Dante And Beatrice

This story is different from the foregoing because these two were historical personalities who lived in Florence, Italy, during the last quarter of the thirteenth century. Dante Alighieri was only nine years old when he fell in love with Beatrice almost the same age as himself. Not much is known about this girl except that she was very fair and beautiful. They saw each other again at the age of eighteen with Beatrice dressed in white. Although Dante was very much in love, he was betrothed to another girl named Gemma whom he married when he was only twelve years old. Beatrice married another man and died at the age of 25. It has been said that the love between Dante and Beatrice was spiritual in character and therefore her death had no deleterious impact on Dante who felt that she was more alive than ever before.

Dante was a poet and considered by many to be the father of Italian poetry. His greatest work was *The Divine Comedy*, a poem in three parts, the *Inferno,* the *Purgatorio,* and the *Paradiso* respectively. The great Italian poet Virgil who lived during the first century B.C guided Dante through Hell and Purgatory. During this tour Dante met many mythological, historical as also contemporary people and observed the torments of a variety of sinners. Virgil could not guide him through the Earthly Paradise because he belonged to a pre-Christian era and therefore supposedly not entitled to receive Grace. Dante found another guide in Beatrice who conducted him through Paradise, purifying him for the final revelation of God. It took him about 14 years to complete the Divine Comedy, which is now considered an allegory charting Dante's own passage from sin and error to a state of Grace. Dante himself had an eventful life during which he was banished from his beloved Florence for a while. But The Divine Comedy ranks among the most esoteric accounts penned by a human being.

Sanyogita And Prithviraj

Theirs was a romance from the 11th century. Prithviraj Chauhan was a dashing young Rajput Prince who extended his kingdom of Ajmer to Rajasthan, Gujerat and Eastern Punjab. His daring exploits and courage became a byword all over Northern India. Sanyogita (some call her Samyukta), the beautiful daughter of Jaichandra Gahawad fell in love with him. Being a resourceful young lady, she found the means to begin a secret poetic correspondence with him. Her father somehow came to know about this and decided to teach his daughter a lesson. He proclaimed a swayamwara for his daughter and invited all the princes of the surrounding kingdoms except Prithviraj. To add insult to injury he made a statue of Prithviraj and kept it as a dwarpala (doorman). On the day of the wedding, Sanyogita walked slowly down the aisle with a garland in her hand. She bypassed all the princes and threw the garland over the statue. At that moment, Prithviraj who was hiding behind the statue quickly put Sanyogita on his horse and galloped away to his capital at Delhi. Jaichandra and his army gave chase but they could not catch up with the dashing couple. Many wars were fought between Sanyogita's husband and her father, for more than a year in which both of them suffered heavily. Nothing more is known about Sanyogita, but Prithviraj himself had no peace in his kingdom as he had to fight against Mahmud Ghori, an invader from Afghanistan. In the first war between them, the Rajputs were victorious and Ghori was brought in chains to Prithviraj who treated his prisoner with respect and courtesy. When Ghori begged for mercy and his liberty, Prithviraj readily released him against the advice of his ministers. But Ghori again attacked the Rajputs. This time the Rajputs were defeated and Prithviraj was brought in chains to Ghori. The proud Rajput stood up straight and looked Ghori in the eye. Ghori ordered him to lower his gaze. Prithviraj in reply, said that a Rajput's eyelids would be lowered only in death, whereupon Ghori ordered that the prisoner's eyes be burnt out with red-hot irons. The blind Prithviraj was brought to court everyday to be taunted by Ghori and his courtiers. Then an archery contest was organised. Although everyone thought it a wild idea, Prithviraj said he would take part if at the contest, Ghori would ask him to shoot. The latter was immediately suspicious but the Rajput King said that this was because he would acquiesce only when an equal asked him to shoot. At the contest, when Ghori asked him to shoot, Prithviraj aimed at the place from where he heard the voice and shot his arrow, killing the Sultan. This is reminiscent of the story in the Bible when the blinded Samson brought down the building in which the Philistines were assembled to mock him.

Padmini, Rani Of Chittor

During the reign of King Ratansen in Mewar, Allah-ud-din was the Sultan of Delhi. He came to know of the beauty of Padmini, Rani of Mewar and wanted to possess her. To this end he pretended that he considered her as a sister and wanted to see her. However, Padmini was wise to his intentions and refused to see him. But her husband persuaded her. She consented on condition that the Sultan could only see her reflection in a mirror. So Allah-ud-din and his entourage came to Chittor and saw the beauty of Padmini. He was so infatuated that he determined to get her by hook or by crook. He pretended to be friendly with her husband. Like all Rajputs, Ratensen was courteous and accompanied the Sultan a little way out of Chittor. The treacherous Sultan kidnapped him and held him for ransom, which was to be Padmini. The Generals of Mewar had a plan. They sent word to the Sultan that they would deliver Padmini and her maidens. Thus150 covered palanquins were sent to Delhi. Out of the palanquins came Rajput warriors armed to the teeth. They quickly rescued Ratansen and rode back to Chittor on horses they obtained from the stables of the Sultan.

The furious Sultan laid siege to Chittor with a huge army. When the supplies in the fort ran out, King Ratensen decided to open the gates and to engage the Muslim army. Padmini and the women in the fort knew that it would be an unequal battle and that the Rajput army would be annihilated. So they built a huge fire and threw themselves in it rather than fall into the hands of the lustful Sultan and his followers. The men, realising they had nothing more to lose, fought to the bitter end until all of them were killed in battle. And thus died a gallant band of Rajputs.

Psychological Jargon Made Intelligible

The Autokinetic Phenomenon

There are hundreds of terms in psychology, which cannot all be looked at here. Hopefully, many important ones can be dealt with in this section. One does not necessarily have to deal with this in an alphabetical order, although I shall begin with the letter A.

I want to start off by defining the Autokinetic Phenomenon and what relationship it has to the concepts of Frames of Reference. Some sixty to seventy years ago, operators in the field of Physiological Psychology performed an important experiment in which a subject was placed in a perfectly dark room. A static pinpoint of light was projected on one of the walls. The task of the subject was to touch the pinpoint of light or to mark its position with a pencil. The experimental subjects ranged over a considerable area of the wall trying to locate the light. Some of them became disoriented and somewhat anxious. Even when the subjects were shown the place where the light was located before the experiment in the fully lit room, the task became extremely difficult once the room became perfectly dark. Psychologists came up with the explanation that every object we perceive is seen in relation to the objects surrounding it. This does not only apply to the perceptual field but also to the conceptual one. Social Psychologists refer to this as the Frames of Reference. Take our thoughts for instance. Every thought leads to a cluster of others related in some way. The Word Association Test devised by Carl Jung made use of this principle. The sophisticated legal system in use, for instance in Australia, is based on the premise that a crime or misdemeanour that a person commits, cannot be seen in isolation but against a series of circumstances surrounding the act. Sometimes even the personality of the offender, namely the cluster of his psychophysiological predispositions, is taken into consideration in determining the punishment or lack of it. Extending this idea to society as a whole, excepting for a few exceptional people, the vast majority can carry on their existence only in relation to others around them. That is how the notion that no man is an island to himself, arose.

Psychologists always talk about schemata, which are clusters of thoughts, ideas and value systems against which a new idea is assessed. If a new idea has to be incorporated, it has to be consonant with the existing schema. Although people say that we all mellow with age, and that our value systems also change accordingly, this is not necessarily what we find in real life. The left-wingers seem to remain rebels with or without a cause, and the rightists remain conservatives throughout their lives.

In the existential sense, this gives rise to the question of attachment to things and to people. It is a significant question whether or not we can give up all kinds of attachment. Some people who have chosen the path of self-abnegation try hard to give up the sense of attachment. For instance among the Catholic Priests and the Swamijis in India it is customary for them to leave the place and people they have been associated with for many years, in obedience to the behests of their superiors. It is not so well known whether they suffer in the process; and if they do, they hide it well. I have been told of a religious teacher who required all those who attended his classes to sit in a different place everyday. To my way of thinking, this is carrying things too far. In this context, attachment and habit are inextricably related. All of us, irrespective of whether we have renounced many things in our life or not, are creatures of habit. We wake up as also go to bed at specific times everyday, we eat our meals at specific times, and we even pray or meditate at given times. In Ashrams and religious institutions punctuality at various activities is insisted upon in a very stringent fashion. In matters of food, those who are vegetarians partake only of certain food items. Some vegetarians avoid garlic; others shun onions and so on. Even non-vegetarians have their pet aversions. If our schedules of life are required to be altered everyday, which the proponents of non-attachment insist upon, there is no end to the anxiety and distress that people will suffer in the process. We live in an orderly universe in which everything seems to occur in a seemingly regular fashion. The sunrise, the sunset, the changing seasons, the tides and so on, are examples.

So what is attachment? Everyone can guess at what it is but it is very difficult to define it. When we get too much in love with people, with things, with money and with other good things in life, we can say that we have become too much attached. In other words, it may not be the love that is to be avoided but the possessiveness that it often engenders. We see this very often when we come across the pathological jealousy of a husband concerning his wife. This kind of irrational emotion has often led to murders. Very many people show their possessiveness in other subtle ways. For example, some people give gifts, which they themselves like, irrespective of what the recipient prefers. These same people think that if they buy expensive gifts, those are appreciated more.

To sum up what has been said above, the Universe is a seamless system, and all its constituents are interlinked. Every event, every person and every thought occurs within the frame of reference of all other systems. All of us are creatures of habit and we continue to follow certain routines day after day. Attachment cannot therefore be avoided. However, too intense an attachment leads to possessiveness, which causes anxiety and distress. When the object which one tries to possess is lost, suffering ensues. Successful living depends on the ability to detach oneself from specific attachments as and when required. Except for those who have renounced everything, it is well nigh impossible to get away from attachments. When we cannot moor objects and thoughts within their proper contexts, disorientation, anxiety and even depression come into being.

Cognitive Dissonance

By way of introduction, I should like to go back in time some five decades when the United States Government Agencies had a massive programme to improve the lot of the subsistence farmers in various parts of the world, particularly in Northern India. The farmers readily undertook to implement the various measures suggested but very soon they went back to their old methods. The originators of the plan could not understand why. To take one example. The vegetarian farmers in one area were helped to initiate poultry keeping which was a very profitable venture in those days. Initially they did make a handsome profit but they soon gave up the project. The planners did not understand that the farmers found it difficult to reconcile their vegetarian way of life to the processing of poultry, however profitable it might have been.

It was in 1957 that Leon Festinger published his *Theory of Cognitive Dissonance,* which turned out to be one of the most influential theories in the field of Social Psychology. He spoke of pairs of relevant cognitions, which could be consonant or dissonant. They are consonant when they are compatible or when one readily follows from the other. They are said to be dissonant when they are incompatible, and can cause discomfort to the person concerned, thus motivating him to reduce the dissonance.

Dissonance can be reduced by one or more of four methods, namely:

1. Removing dissonant cognitions

2. Adding new consonant cognitions

3. Reducing the importance of dissonant cognitions, or

4. Increasing the importance of consonant cognitions

Festinger himself gave the example of a heavy smoker who is informed that smoking is bad for the lungs. If he continues to smoke, this is dissonant with the information he has received. He could then:

1. Stop smoking, which is consonant with the cognition (knowledge) that smoking is harmful, or

2. He could change his cognition (knowledge) and believe that smoking does no damage to his health and therefore continue smoking, or

3. He might believe that the risk to health from smoking is negligible compared with other dangers in modern living. He could also emphasise the enjoyment he derives from smoking, or

4. He might look for positive cognitions, namely that smoking reduces tension and prevents weight gain.

In a very interesting book entitled "The Ugly American," Jim Lederer one of the most influential journalists in the USA, has given examples of how the Americans have been misguided in their zeal to modernise the world. Without paying any attention to the question of dissonance in human affairs, they have gone about merrily trying to introduce so-called modernisation programmes into cultures, which are not ready to embrace them. Lederer also gives examples of how in many of the so-called third world countries people are able to make do with the materials they have at hand to repair sophisticated machinery. Thus we find that in many areas of India, local motor mechanics can improvise or modify the materials they have, to effect repairs.

Cognitive Dissonance is very important when dealing with the problems of young Indian children, born and brought up in Australia. In the classroom and in the sports field they come into contact with value systems and cultural norms, which are alien to those of their parents. Then a conflict arises as to who they are and what kind of behavioural systems they should emulate. The foremost thing that comes to mind is the question of religious observances that Indian parents try to teach their children. When they go to the Hindu temple, they see so many images, which the Westerners think, are innumerable Gods. Many Indian children cannot immediately grasp the fact that the images are not really Gods but are there to help them visualise the Deity. The rituals they see in the Temple seem strange to them, especially if they have been to Christian Churches in company with their classmates. Many Indian children rebel against the worship patterns of their parents. Some even lose their faith in God. Perceptive parents would not immediately condemn their offspring but they would try to reduce the dissonance by whatever cognitions available to them. Intellectual arguments may not be of much avail because many dissonant cognitions are resolved by the process of rationalisation. It might be recalled that Rationalisation is an unconscious device whereby a human being attempts to explain away unacceptable behaviour, giving a plausible excuse for his/her decisions.

Adolescent boys and girls in the throes of their sexual awakening may have to deal with many social institutions of the Western Culture, as for instance the dating behaviour made much of, here. Then there are things like being able to stay out late at night. But it must be said to the credit of many Asian boys and girls that they are able to keep these things in abeyance until they have completed their schooling.

One of the very important aspects of life, which can cause a great deal of dissonance, is the choice of clothes to wear. The adolescent girl may think she has to keep up with her peers by wearing, for instance, a miniskirt. Even adult women sometimes choose to go to work in "dresses" because they think otherwise they may not be respected. Men too are shy about being seen in public wearing a dhoti. I think we have a great deal to learn from our Swamijis who take pride in wearing our national dress, despite the vagaries of climate in this country.

The poor people of India have a very efficient way of resolving dissonance at least in some aspects. About 35 years ago, when the Point 4 Programme of the USA was operating in India, some social scientists worked in a Development Bloc near New Delhi. The population in this area consisted of Vegetarian Jats, who were so poor that they could eat only one full meal a day. This had been going on for generations. They became used to the massive cars the USA project officers drove to work. In one of the questionnaires, the villagers were asked: "Would you like to have one of these big cars that you see everyday?" Almost to a man, they all said "No". When asked why not, they replied that in this life it was unrealistic of them to think of possessing a car. It would only make them miserable to think about it!

Finally the question arises as to whether a human being can avoid dissonant cognitions altogether. All thinking people, by the very nature of their life patterns, have to come across cognitive dissonance and conflict in their lives. I might even go as far as to say that the resolution of dissonant cognitions adds spice to our lives. Otherwise we would not have paid ombudsmen, trouble-shooters and politicians. These people thrive on helping others to resolve cognitive dissonance. At least they say so!

Subliminal Perception:

Every instant the human organism is bombarded by millions of stimuli. It stands to reason that a person cannot perceive or react to all of them. In fact there is a kind of filtering mechanism in our brain which enables us to become aware of only those things in the environment which are of primary importance to us, or which represent a threat to our safety and well being. Thus there may be degrees of awareness of our environment. Some stimuli could receive instant attention. Some others may be perceived and dismissed as non-essential. There may yet be others, which the organism has no awareness of having perceived at all.

The word *limen* means threshold. Subliminal perception occurs when very weak stimuli reaching the organism result in lack of awareness. This phenomenon achieved wide notice after a claim by the market researcher James Vicary in 1957 of an experiment he conducted at a movie theatre in Fort Lee, New Jersey. Over a six-week period some 45,700 patrons who attended the theatre were shown two messages, **Eat Popcorn** and **Drink Coca-Cola** while they watched the film **Picnic.** These messages were flashed for 3/1000 of a second once every five seconds. This duration was so short that the patrons were not aware of having perceived the messages. However, Vicary claimed that the sales of popcorn rose by 57.7% and that of Coca-Cola by 18% over the six-week period when the study was in progress. Although later he withdrew his claim as a fabrication, it aroused worldwide interest.

Vance Packard, in his book **The Hidden Persuaders** deals with the many ways in which advertisers try to get at the public so that the wares they promote could be sold easily. The whole point of Subliminal Advertising is to get the consumer to buy things without knowing why he or she seems impelled to purchase the product in question. However, there is a great deal of controversy regarding subliminal perception, whether or not it really works. Fearful members of the public are apprehensive that they could be manipulated into behaving in ways, which they would not normally do without this kind of subliminal input. Autocratic regimes have always been researching means whereby they could obtain compliance from the general public with or without their awareness. The irrational fear of communism and communists that has always existed in the United States of America is an example of how the state can influence the thinking of its citizens. At one time when McCarthyism was rife in the States, innocent citizens were deprived of their privileges and even their freedom on the impression that they were communists. Paul Robeson, the great bass singer and actor was one of those who suffered intensely because of this prejudice. In his case he was also a black man, which made it worse. At one stage his passport was even impounded because he dared to say that there was greater respect for black people in the Soviet Union than in the United States. However, in those cases people were aware of the fact that the State had a definite agenda on hand.

One of the present day uses of subliminal messages is in the audiotapes produced by some proponents of Creative Visualisation who claim to have introduced subliminal messages of welfare and positive thinking among the various natural sounds of the forest and of the water falling. Many people still doubt these claims. Some even doubt there are really subliminal messages incorporated into these tapes. The trouble is that the investigator has no way of telling that there are indeed subliminal messages embedded in these tapes. Many such tapes for self-help claim to cure a variety of problems like smoking, obesity and stress. Others lay claims for the increase in memory efficiency, speed of learning and the development of various skills at tennis or golf or basketball. One of the most extraordinary claims was made by William Bryan Keys who says that the word *sex* was often embedded in advertisements. In his book ***Subliminal Seduction and Media Sexploitation*** published in 1970 he gives many examples of products such as crackers and soft drinks where such words relating to sex have been embedded. Although these words are not consciously perceived, their unconscious perception can elicit sexual arousal, which makes the products more attractive to consumers. However, this is an area, which remains largely unexplored. All this takes us back to the theory of the *Id* formulated by Sigmund Freud in the early part of the last century. Subliminal perception is thought to be an easy avenue to the Id where impressions and thoughts are accepted without questioning.

Sometimes learning can take place when there are non-subliminal stimuli in the background. Those who have read the book ***Cheaper by the Dozen*** would remember that the efficiency expert in question helped his children learn many languages by having loudspeakers installed in every room of the house including the toilet. Even when they were not aware of deliberately learning, they were listening to language instruction over the audio system. It has been claimed that in six months they became proficient in at least three languages other than their native English. Following this momentous experiment, there was a flurry of interest in sleep learning in which tape recorders were placed under the pillows when a person was about to go to sleep. The tapes played included many self-improvement ones on memory and speed of learning. However, the interest in these petered out when there seemed to be little evidence that these produced positive learning. However, at Behavioural Medicine Associates run by Benjamin Wolman and Montague Ullman in the USA, they have begun to employ a subliminal videotape to help clients relax before biofeedback or hypnotic sessions. These videotapes contain a colourful kaleidoscope together with subliminal phrases of relaxation and good feeling.

There have been many studies on the feasibility of subliminal perception. In some studies, the subject of the experiment was connected to various kinds of apparatus to measure autonomic responses like blood pressure, skin conductance, EEG and EMG. When emotion-laden words were presented at subliminal levels, the person consciously denied having perceived the messages; however, the autonomic responses indicated otherwise, demonstrating that at an unconscious level these messages were apprehended.

Although subliminal perception continues to cause antagonism in certain quarters, it has been used as a tool in the treatment of eating disorders and especially in phobias with very good results. It has been found that all the sensory modalities are susceptible to subliminal influences. An interesting finding is that subliminal olfactory stimuli can have very great influence in human behaviour. Even though male subjects may not be able to detect consciously the smell of female ***pheromones***, when these are present, the subjects seem to consider the photographs of women as being more attractive than they would have been otherwise. To refresh the memory of readers, ***pheromones*** are body smells that are not consciously detected but which affect the behaviour of others towards the person giving off these chemical signals.

The ancient Hindu people must have been aware of the possibility of subliminal learning. One example is the custom of whispering in the ears of a baby its name. It is not known how this custom originated and as to how the baby is supposed to become aware of the meaning of its name.

No other culture has studied consciousness and awareness as much as the Indians have done over more than three to four millennia. Even if they have not done experiments as have been done in the West, their intuitive knowledge of these things was very vast indeed. There are more words to denote different types of consciousness in Sanskrit than in any other languages of the world.

Like sleep, there may be some other types of consciousness in which external stimulation does not elicit any responses. One such state is Samadhi in which the senses are under perfect control and perhaps turned inwards which makes a person oblivious of all that goes on around him. I am sure most people are aware of the story of King Parikshit who came across saint Samika in the forest. The saint was in a deep state of meditation. The King not being aware of the nature of Samadhi, asked the saint for a drink of water. When Samika did not respond in any way, the king, in a rage, picked up a dead snake, which was lying nearby and draped it around the neck of the saint. Seeing this, the Saint's son invoked a curse on the king whereby he would be bitten by a snake and die within seven days. The king was then enabled, by listening to various saints, to obtain the Wisdom of God before he died at the end of the period. There could perhaps be variants of Samadhi in which subliminal or supraliminal stimuli can elicit appropriate responses.

It had often been thought that when a person undergoes deep anaesthesia, he/she is oblivious of anything that happened during the operation. Direct questioning afterwards does not elicit positive answers but by indirect methods like asking him/her to complete a sentence, it has been found that patients do remember some snatches of conversation carried on by the surgical staff.

Our present knowledge is not perhaps extensive enough to categorise the varieties of stimuli, their limits of exposure and the consequent degree of awareness evoked. Sometimes incidental learning takes place without a person paying attention to a particular situation. I am sure many of us may have had this experience of going to a shopping centre to buy something. Months or even years later, when we need a special object, we have the awareness that it will be found in a particular area although on the first occasion we had had no idea of its presence there.

If subliminal perception is possible, then there is no limit to the applications it can have in the lives of human beings. There is nothing in the world that cannot be learned and there would be no end to the self-improvement, which can be achieved.

Claustrophobia

A phobia is a common name for an irrational fear. One of most common phobias is Claustrophobia the fear of being in an enclosed space like a lift or a small room or an aeroplane. Claustrophobics are constantly on the search for an escape route. For instance on entering a room or hallway the sufferer will search for the door and place himself/herself as near to it as possible. Car journeys become difficult particularly if they require travel on a motorway. Those suffering from this phobia might also avoid the rush hour to avoid getting trapped in a traffic jam. Hospital checks involving scans where the patient is slowly moved through the machine become impossible without heavy sedatives. If one lives or works in an upper floor, the lifts are usually avoided, a person with this phobia electing to climb several flights of stairs. Even a large room, if filled with people, will pose a threat unless the person can position himself near a doorway. Claustrophobia is an extreme case of an anxiety attack. The symptoms can include sweating, accelerated heart rate, hyperventilation, light-headedness, nausea and fainting. Once a person has experienced a number of anxiety attacks, he becomes increasingly afraid of experiencing another. So the habit is established of avoidance of objects or situations that bring on the attack. This makes the claustrophobia worse. The aetiology of this phobia is sometimes clear and sometimes it is not. For instance, the claustrophobia of a young man had its origin when as a young boy he was caught under the flooring of his house and it was a few minutes before he was rescued. In his case, the condition developed slowly until it reached phenomenal proportions. Another little girl was punished for some minor infringement of discipline, her father locking her up in a closet for half an hour or so. She developed a severe type of claustrophobia that nearly crippled her.

A clinical psychologist usually carries out the treatment of claustrophobia although the psychiatrist or the general practitioner may prescribe tranquillisers and antidepressants. Drugs known as beta-blockers may also be used to treat the physical symptoms of anxiety. But the treatment of choice is psychological.

First, there is a method known as Flooding in which the patient is exposed to the phobic object (under supervision by the psychologist) and kept in that situation until the overwhelming anxiety attack passes. This type of treatment should be attempted only by an experienced clinical psychologist as otherwise there is the chance of exacerbation of the symptoms and of the increase in anxiety.

The best treatment for this condition is known as Systematic Desensitisation, which is carried out in a graduated series of steps. At first the person is taught relaxation and visualisation. Then a list known as the Fear Hierarchy is constructed which consists of fear evoking stimuli starting from items of low intensity anxiety to those of intense anxiety. While the patient is relaxed, the mildest anxiety-evoking item is introduced in imagination. After visualising this for sometime, when the anxiety evoked is extinguished, the next higher stimulus is required to be imagined. The Anxiety is then extinguished because of the relaxation response. By doing this in a systematic manner, the anxiety evoked by the intense stimulus is extinguished. What is more, when the person comes in contact with the actual stimulus itself, he/she will be able to go through the experience with the least amount of anxiety. Regular practice like this will get rid of the anxiety. It is usual for treatment to be carried on for about 8 to 10 bi-weekly sessions.

One of the latest methods of dealing with this problem is by Cognitive Behaviour Therapy in which the patient is encouraged to confront and change the specific thoughts and attitudes that lead to the feelings of fear.

Modelling is another method in which the patient watches other people confronting the feared object without fear, thereby his own fear being lessened.

Logotherapy:

The late Viktor E. Frankl a Professor of Neurology and Physiology at the University of Vienna Medical School was the originator of this method of Therapy. It might be recalled that in Vedanta philosophy, the word termed Vak has more or less the same connotation as Logos or meaning. The first chapter of St, John's Gospel begins thus: "In the beginning was the Word, and the Word was with God, and the Word was God." The Chambers's Dictionary defines Logos as in the Stoic philosophy, the active principle living in and determining the world.

In various conditions like alcoholism, addiction or depression, the sufferer has a feeling of aimlessness and emptiness. In other words there is the loss of meaning to life. Logotherapy is useful for those conditions as also for phobias, anxiety, and obsessive-compulsive disorders.

Basically this is an existentialist method as it emphasises the primacy of the freedom of the will and the consequent shouldering of responsibility. It will be recalled that Freud emphasised the will to pleasure that all human beings have, and Adler referred to the will to power. Meaning is unique to every individual and must be discovered during the process of living. Frankl's logotherapy also holds that whatever the state of the world, our attitude can always help us. The interpretations that men place on events are more important than the events themselves. Many people who shared the death camps with Frankl even when facing death and unimaginable suffering turned their situation into a supremely meaningful one by their courage and steadfastness. Frankl spent three years in Auschwitz and Dachau and the things he learned about suffering and the search for meaning led to his promulgation of logotherapy as the method of choice in some aspects of psychotherapy.

A technique referred to as Paradoxical Intention is central to logotherapy. This is the method whereby the therapist encourages the patient to intently wish for precisely what he/she fears. The following example will make this clear. A middle-aged woman who developed the fear of germs was encouraged to wash her hands many times till they became raw. The therapist let her go down on all fours and scrub the floor of the hospital again and again. He made a game of it and he encouraged the woman to touch doorknobs and other objects that she had originally thought were contaminated. When she forced herself to do all these things her phobia disappeared, and so did her compulsion to wash.

There is another device called Dereflection in which the therapist diverts the attention of his client away from his/her problems towards something meaningful. This appears to be commonsense but it does work because the mind cannot remain a vacuum for any length of time. Brooding over problems is the sign of an anxious person but when a positive or creative thought is substituted, it does make him/her happy and fulfilled.

The therapist then tries to orient the patient's discernment of meaning, in the past in the present and in the future. This means careful analysis of the person's whole life, his memories, his dreams, his aspirations and what would create meaning to his life. Unlike psychoanalysis, Logotherapy is directive and therefore takes considerably less time than other types of therapy. Therefore it seems to address dimensions of life not taken into account in other methods. Moreover it is very simple to understand. Those who have been brought up in the free associations methods usually think Logotherapy is authoritarian and too religious to stand the rigors of scientific analysis. In my opinion the training in the freedom of will is the greatest strength of Frankl's therapy.

Amnesia

Whenever there is a partial or complete loss of memory, this condition is referred to as Amnesia. There are two main causes for amnesia, physical and psychological. Among the physical causes are, traumatic injury to the brain caused by a blow to the head for example, a brain tumour or a swelling on the brain. There are innumerable psychological traumata that can cause amnesia. Sometimes these are referred to as Hysterical Amnesia (or Fugue Amnesia).

I wish to give here a case study in which brain damage and emotional trauma contributed to the amnesic condition. This is the story of a 20 year-old White

Caucasian girl who had had a very strict upbringing by devout Catholic parents. Let us call her Samantha. It was only when she was 19 years old that she had her first boy friend. She was a much sought after girl not only because of her physical attractiveness but also because of her sunny disposition. The young man who took her fancy seemed to love her very much, but like most young men, after a while he began to insist that they have a sexual relationship. She was averse to the idea, but at the same time she was afraid that he might stop seeing her if she persisted in denying him what he wanted. Samantha also knew that her parents, especially her mother, would be horrified if she began a sexual relationship with her boyfriend. As her twentieth birthday approached, her boyfriend suggested that they go away together for a weekend to Coffs Harbour where his parents lived. Samantha was torn between her moral standards and the need to please her boyfriend. With great difficulty she was able to confide in her mother who was at a loss to know how best to counsel her daughter. In the meanwhile the boyfriend went ahead with arrangements for the weekend.

At this stage, it is necessary to say something about his car. Some three decades ago when all this happened, most cars had bench seats in front and no seat belts. In this particular car the front passenger side door had a tendency to fly open whenever it ran over rough terrain. Tony had promised to get the door repaired but he had not done so even on the day the young couple was to depart on their holiday. Samantha's father, in the meanwhile, knew nothing about these plans. So, it was the mother who saw them off. She noticed that her daughter looked drawn and tense; contrary to what young people usually do, she was sitting away from her boyfriend and close to the door. At the best of times Tony was a rash driver. When they reached a clear stretch of road, he put his foot down on the accelerator. The left side door flew open and Samantha was thrown on the road. She was badly hurt, as she had landed almost on her head. After preliminary treatment at the local hospital, which was ill equipped to deal with such a serious case, she was flown to a well-known teaching hospital in Sydney. She lay in a deep coma for three weeks after which she drifted in and out of unconsciousness for a few more days. When she finally regained consciousness, a comprehensive rehabilitation programme was worked out.

As soon as she was well enough to undergo psychological tests, the therapist administered cognitive tests, which would indicate not only the extent of brain damage she had suffered but also estimate what her intellectual level might have been before the accident. It came out that she had suffered substantial damage to the frontal lobes of the brain, which would cause some loss of inhibitions and affect her planning ability. Usually after a serious accident such as the one that

Samantha had suffered, some loss of memory was likely. This amnesia can be of two kinds; in ***anterograde amnesia***, memory of events sometime ***after*** the accident is lost. The second kind of amnesia is ***retrograde amnesia*** in which the patient loses a chunk of memory of events ***before*** the accident. A victim rarely remembers the accident itself. In Samantha's case, she had amnesia for 8 years from 11 to 19 years of her life, which was very unusual.

Week by week she improved in her cognitive ability, but the retrograde amnesia for 8 years remained. Sometimes amnesia caused by emotional causes can be removed by a method known as ***abreaction.*** This is a process whereby re-living of a traumatic event causes a flood of emotion at the end of which the subject appears to obtain a great deal of relief. An intravenous injection of the so-called truth drug Sodium Pentothal is administered to start the abreaction. Sometimes it can also be performed under hypnosis. I do not think these days psychiatrists perform abreaction for the simple reason that it entails a lot of time and the attendance of a psychiatrist together with a clinical psychologist and perhaps a social worker to guide the course of the process. Moreover, all the things that the subject says in an abreaction need not necessarily be the truth. When the drug was administered, Samantha began to cry and to relate how she hated to go to the Convent School as a boarder at the age of 11. The discipline at that school was very strict and the living conditions Spartan. Excepting for one young nun, all the others seemed aloof and uncaring. Samantha said she did not know how she was able to spend those eight years. This abreaction took about two and a half hours and exact records of it were kept. The strange thing was that when Samantha came out of the influence of the drug she had again forgotten her experiences during the eight years in question. Two more abreactions were performed at weekly intervals with the same result. Samantha was able to express her anger at her boyfriend for his insistence on a sexual relationship. During the third session she became very calm and she had decided to break off her relationship with her boyfriend. But her amnesia for the eight years returned when the effects of the drug wore off. The somewhat massive brain damage she had suffered could have been responsible for this condition. Samantha's rehabilitation was a success in that she was able to go back to work. Soon she met and married another young man. The next year she brought her month-old-son to the hospital and she seemed happily settled in her life.

Sometimes a bump on the head could cause amnesia for a few hours. A very tall and rather stout young woman bought a Morris Mini Minor, which was all of a rage in those days. It is not clear why she bought such a small car as getting in and out of it was a great difficulty for her. One day while driving along to work in the morning, she had to brake suddenly. She bumped her head on the roof of the car. There was no pain or concussion. Yet, in the evening when she returned home, she found she could not remember anything that had happened during the day. On another occasion the same young woman found herself sitting on the steps of the hospital in Randwick early on a Monday morning. She had no recollection of how she came to be there or what she had done during the weekend. The case history of this young woman is rather interesting if it weren't so sad. She was the eldest among her siblings. Her parents had had a stormy relationship and the mother made it clear to her that she was not planned nor wanted. Although she was a very intelligent girl she felt this rejection very sorely and started to overeat. Very soon she began to put on weight until she had become enormous. Despite the ostracism by her peers at school, she passed her H.S.C. with good marks. Getting a job was a problem for her. When she made enquiries by telephone, the people at the other end were impressed because of her excellent speaking voice and diction. But when she appeared at the interview they would take one look at her and say that they were sorry, as the position had already been filled. It was with great difficulty she obtained a job in a factory. But she had no social life to speak of. Because of her feelings of rejection by the world at large, many people began to take advantage of her. She became an unmarried mother. Her problems with amnesia could perhaps be seen as a survival device engineered by her mind to enable her to forget the misery in her life.

Indian literature and mythology use images of binding, chaining and captivity as synonymous with forgetting, which should be of interest to us. Thus forgetting of incidents and relationships happens due to many circumstances. For instance there is the story of the Yogi who happened to fall in love with a beautiful queen. Infatuated by her beauty he forgot his true identity. He lived with her in her palace. One of the Yogi's devoted students while making his customary trip to the spirit world, got knowledge of his master's enslavement which would result in his death due to the forgetfulness of his duties. The student searched the Book of Fates, found the leaf, which contained the destiny of his Guru and erased his name from the list of the dead. Knowing with his eye of understanding that the Queen lived in Ceylon, the student rushed there, disguised himself as a dancing girl and sang sweetly to his master about his former life. Gradually the memory of what he was, dawned on the Yogi and he understood that his infatuation was a forgetfulness of his true and immortal nature. Thus he was enabled to return to his former purity of life

Sometimes the curse of a Maharishi can cause amnesia in the life of a person. The story of Shakuntala is an instance in point. She was the daughter of Viswamitra and Menaka. Soon after her birth, her parents abandoned her in the forest where the sage Kanwa found her and brought her up as his own daughter. She grew up to be a beautiful maiden. One day she met King Dushyanta who had been hunting in the forest. For both of them it was love at first sight and they were married by the Gandharva rite. The king gave her a ring before he left and told her to come to him as soon as possible. Shakuntala being preoccupied with thoughts of her husband did not realise that the sage Durvasa had come to the Ashram. When she did not immediately greet him with the respect that he expected, he cursed her saying that the person she was thinking about would completely forget her. Shakuntala begged his forgiveness. He relented somewhat and said that although he could not revoke his curse, there was one proviso he could make which would make Shakuntala's husband recollect all that he had forgotten if she could produce a token, that he could recognise as his own. Unfortunately she had lost the ring while bathing in the river. Her mother Menaka took her and the son born to her, to her own residence and looked after them. In the meanwhile, a fisherman had caught the fish that had swallowed the ring and realising that it belonged to the King, he had taken it to the palace. The moment the King caught sight of the ring he remembered Shakuntala. Grief-stricken, he searched for her all over the three worlds until he found her. The dynamics of how a curse like this can cause amnesia is not very clear. We can only put it down to the power of focussed spiritual energy.

When we consider our own temporal existence on the face of this earth, we have to accept that most of us are operating under a cloud of amnesia about our real nature. We are being influenced by the phenomena around us and imagine that these seemingly pleasant experiences constitute reality. Such is the beguiling nature of Maya. This amnesia can be eliminated only when we realise our true nature as being the possessors of the divine Atman free from all taints of impurity.

Personality and Renunciation

For the purpose of this presentation I have chosen to use the Jungian classification of personality. It might be recalled that the Swiss Psychiatrist Carl Gustav Jung presented two personality types, which he referred to as Extraverted and Introverted. The ancient Indians and the Chinese too were familiar with this dichotomy and they had their own systems to represent it. A working knowledge of these concepts may be useful here. Although the words *introverted* and *extroverted* have been current in our vocabulary for a very long time, laymen, as also professional people, are not very clear as to what these might mean in terms of human experience.

We can perhaps postulate a personality continuum with extroversion at one end and introversion at the other. However, it has to be realised that pure introverts or pure extroverts are statistical abstractions, most people having characteristics of both.

Jung delineated the extroverted person as being object-oriented and the introvert as being subjective. It is, however, possible for a person to be extroverted on some occasions and introverted on others. Jung went on to say that the unconscious of an introvert is extroverted and that the unconscious of an extrovert is introverted respectively. There is a parallel here with the concepts of Kundalini Yoga, which postulates the Ida and Pingala, representing the feminine and masculine aspects respectively. In the Chinese system these are referred to as Yin and Yang respectively.

Further Jung postulated four psychological functions namely thinking, feeling, sensation and intuition. Thinking and Feeling were considered rational functions, and intuition and sensation as irrational functions.

It was Pavlov, in his study of conditioning, who postulated the concept of simultaneous cortical excitation and inhibition, the balance of which determined the conditionability of his dogs. The late Professor H.J.Eysenck, one of the foremost psychologists the world has ever known, advanced the hypothesis that some human beings have predominance of cortical excitation, at the same time manifesting behavioural inhibition. These are the introverted people. Those who showed a predominance of cortical inhibition are the extroverts.

The Ascending Reticular Activating System (ARAS) situated in the brain stem, has been considered to play an important part in wakefulness, alertness, vigilance and in the regulation of sensory input. Eysenck has suggested that there could be a physiological (and genetic) basis for personality. Extroversion-Introversion is closely related to the habitual arousal level of the cortex. We get tense and wound up, highly aroused before an important examination, but we are relaxed and drowsy late in the evening in front of the television.

The brain functions best at moderately high levels of arousal. Introverts have higher habitual levels of arousal than extroverts do, which is why they tend to be better at learning, conditioning and remembering.

The cortex also has the function of keeping the lower levels of the brain in check, which is why the behaviour of introverts is more inhibited than that of extroverts. Alcohol (a central nervous system depressant) makes people more extroverted, whereas amphetamines, which are stimulant drugs, have the opposite effect. They make people more introverted. Therefore, by giving people depressant or stimulant drugs we can alter the physical basis of their personality and thus their behaviour.

Prolific laboratory and social experimentation to validate the theory of Introversion-Extroversion, has brought out some very interesting findings. Some of these are:

- Introverts have higher levels of cortical arousal, better ability to form conditioned responses and seem to be better learners using the formal direct teaching methods.

- Introverts are more susceptible to punishment.

- The body temperature of introverts is higher in the morning and early afternoon

- They do not normally suffer from boredom.

- They seek stimulus avoidance, are cautious, have a lower threshold to pain and tend to be oversocialised.

- They are process-oriented, tend to avoid competitive situations and have a rich fantasy life.

- The threshold for pain is lower for the introvert and therefore it may be found that he suffers disproportionately to the degree of intensity of the stimulation, which causes it.

- Introverts may be seen to show stimulus aversion in the sense that they already have a high cortical arousal, any further stimulation being perceived as unpleasant. It is perhaps the introversive characteristic of the reclusive Yogi, which enables him to spend a massive slice of his life ensconced in a cave oblivious to the hustle and bustle of city life.

- One of the interesting outcomes is the tendency of introverts towards process-orientation, which may have been responsible for the ancient sages of India to postulate the theory of Karma involving rebirth thousands or millions of times until the individual Atman is ready to merge with the Divine Consciousness.

- There are many practical considerations, which have to be taken into account at this stage. Introverted people seem to function best in the forenoon. As the day progresses, their body temperatures and their efficiency tend to wane, whereas extroverted people come alive in the late afternoon. It is interesting to note that in Vedanta and Yoga philosophies, 3 a.m., referred to as Brahma Muhurtam (or the time of Brahma) is said to be the best time for contemplation and study.

- Extroverts, on the other hand, have a craving for stimulation, often need change of activity, and rest pauses, and are very susceptible to rewards. They are impulsive and are slower to learn the rules of society.

Maharishi Patanjali, one of the celebrated sages of India, has enumerated eight steps designed to enable a person to actualise himself/herself. Out of these, the fifth step is referred to as Pratyahara, meaning the act of turning inwards and withdrawal from the senses. A fanciful example given in Hindu Scriptures is that of a tortoise withdrawing its legs and head into its shell. Meditation seems to be a device for turning inwards.

It has been said that introverts are very complex people with many contradictions in their nature. Many of them do not find it difficult to hold opposing ideas in their consciousness. Some psychologists hold that this kind of Janusian thinking makes for creativity and is very much a right hemisphere characteristic. The gifted people who put together the Upanishads were certainly inward looking. Introverts, because of their greater conditionability learn the rules of society much quicker than their extroverted brethren do. There is some evidence that inward-looking people seem to have an intense libido, which makes them easily attracted to the members of the opposite sex. At the same time the capacity for looking within causes the development of a very stringent superego (Conscience), which imposes a rigorous moral value. It is therefore not difficult to infer that introverted people may have an internal struggle to keep their libido within moral bounds.

In this context it is important to remember that some of the celebrated Maharishis known to ancient Indians and who used to engage in severe Tapas (austerities), did acquire enormous powers to challenge even the Gods. So, the Gods used to send down Apsaras in the shape of beautiful young women to tempt them. At first the Maharishi would resist the attractions of their senses, but in the end, their libido would win out. Their transitory indulgence in sensual pleasures would deplete their powers. Then they had to start all over again. Coming to comparatively modern times, Gandhi and Tolstoy who sought to walk in the paths of spiritual awakening, were very susceptible to the meretricious power of the senses.

One of the important things about introversion is that it endows the person who has it, with insight into the personality predilections of people around him, enabling him to switch roles in a facile manner. Therefore introverted people can be good actors. This is not to say that all of then can be a success on the silver screen. For every introverted Sir Lawrence Olivier, there are hundreds of others whose social inhibitions keep them very much earth-bound.

Humour is another thing that comes easily to the introvert. Not that in a social context he could become the life and soul of the party, but there is certainly the capacity to chuckle inwardly or even to laugh outright, especially while reading a book. Introverted people seem to be fond of cartoons of the Walt Disney kind. Those who make those cartoons are perhaps introverted as well.

Now we come to the heart of the matter. The Bhagavad-Gita, which is the Bible for the majority of the Hindus describes important ways in which the Sadhaka can get release from the meretricious hold of Karmas and attain Mukti or union with the Absolute. Lord Krishna postulated two important ways in which this can be done, by Karma Yoga and Karma Sanyasa. Karma Yoga can be simply said to be the act of living in this world with the consecration of all actions and their fruits to the Divine. This means that a householder has only to change his attitude towards actions but this does not mean renunciation of all the things of the world. The renunciation in this case is not the giving up of any activities but only the giving up of attachment towards them. Then there is Karma Sanyasa. This is one of the most difficult concepts to understand. But it is clear that the Bhagavad Gita says that it is the ultimate in renunciation. We read that Lord Krishna said to Arjuna: "The real Sanyasi is he who does not desire one thing or hate another. The word Sanyasa can well be applied to work done without regard to success or failure, profit or loss, honour or dishonour, to any activity engaged in, as offering to the Lord. Mere inactivity announced by the gerua cloth and the shaved head is no Sanyasa at all. He who has avoided the duality of joy and grief, of good and bad, he alone deserves the name. So better than the giving up of Karma, is the renunciation of the fruits of actions; it also yields greater joy....Therefore, of these two, Sanyasa and Karma Yoga, whichever is followed, the fruit of the other too can be won. For there is Ananda in Karma: there is Ananda too in Renunciation." It is clear then that whereas in Sanyasa, Karma Yoga is implicit, we cannot say that the path of Karma Yoga implies all the characteristics of Sanyasa.

In my opinion, Jesus was a great Karma Sanyasi, who lived two thousand odd years ago. If we look at his life we shall find that his personality and renunciation pattern fulfil the requirements amply. First of all, he had no possessions or even a permanent place to live in. When a man came and said to him "Master, I will follow thee whithersover thou goest" Jesus said to him "The foxes have holes and the birds of the air have nests; but the Son of man hath nowhere to lay his head." We have also to make a distinction here between Ego that most human beings have and the complete awareness of Jesus that he was divine. He said simply "I and the Father are One." Some of his sayings were mystical and difficult to understand. For instance, "I am the resurrection and the life. He who believeth in me, though he were dead, yet shall he live. He who liveth and believeth in me shall never die." His infinite compassion for human beings is exemplified by his invitation, "Come unto me all ye that labour and are heavy laden and I will give you rest." In St. John's Gospel there is one incident reported as to how he dealt with sin in the case of human beings. A woman caught in adultery was brought by a mob to Jesus. The punishment for such behaviour in the Jewish code at that time was death by stoning. Jesus who was sitting on the floor did not even look up. He said, "He who is without sin cast the first stone." When he looked up again, there was only this woman standing there. All her accusers had disappeared, being convicted by their own conscience! He said to her simply, "Go and sin no more." This incident illustrates how a Sanyasi looks at human foibles. He never makes any kind of judgments about people. Although he lived among human beings, eating and drinking and partaking of the social life of the community, he did not take these things as important. Many a time, his disciples mistook his reference to food as physical sustenance, whereas he was speaking about the food for the soul. He was able to fast forty days and forty nights, spending his time in deep meditation in the wilderness.

He let himself be put to the test by Satan who brought forward very attractive allurements. Of course he easily turned these down because his focus was always on the mission his father had entrusted to him. He was aware that the greatest gift that a human being can give to another is the gift of life. He said," Greater love hath no man than this, that a man lay down his life for his friends." He had mastered the art of infinite love for the whole of mankind without any attachments whatsoever. This aspect is the ultimate in Sanyasa. On one occasion when his mother Mary who is considered to be the embodiment of innocence and purity came to see him, he said to her "Woman what have I to do with thee? My hour is not yet come." And yet he loved his mother. When he was about to depart his body he said to his mother; "Woman behold thy son" referring to his favourite disciple who was standing by. He said to him: 'Behold thy mother." He believed as all Sanyasis do, that God looks after all his children. This passage from St. Matthew's gospel is the quintessence of existence. He said "Take no thought for your life, what ye shall eat or what ye shall drink; nor yet for your body, what ye shall put on. Is not the life more than meat and the body than raiment? Behold the fowls of the air; for they sow not, neither do they reap, nor gather into barns: yet your heavenly Father feedeth them. Are ye not much better than they?...Consider the lilies of the field, how they grow; they toil not, neither do they spin: And yet I say unto you, that even Solomon in all his glory was not arrayed like one of these." One of the insightful experiences of the Sanyasi is that he is able to pierce the veil of Maya and to get at the reality behind it. Jesus often spoke about his kingdom and this was difficult for the people around him to understand. For them a kingdom meant royal apparel, a palace and thousands of servants and soldiers. The Jews of the time expected the Messiah to fight his enemies and to establish an earthly kingdom. So he said: "My kingdom is not of this world."

It might be remembered that the fifth step in Maharashi Patanjali's eightfold path of Yoga is known as Pratyahara which when translated into English means the act of turning inwards. A sanyasi whenever he goes into deep Samadhi can be said to go into the trance state of pratyahara, which is what Jesus did very often in his life on earth. All introverted people have the ability to turn inwards. By this token we can say that Jesus was an introverted person. To the uninitiated this characteristic of Jesus is very hard to understand. This is because he lived among people sharing their lives very intimately, eating and drinking and socialising with them. Many Maharishis have done the same thing including Ramakrishna Paramahansa. It has to be emphasised that Sanyasis on the whole have abrogated the Ego almost to the point of extinction, since their identification with the

Divine is complete. Why they still remain in the flesh is because they choose to help ordinary human beings in their quest for enlightenment.

The Karma Yogi also has chosen his goal as the attainment of the Divine but his methods remain somewhat different from that of the Karma Sanyasi. His renunciation pattern is also somewhat different. His main renunciation is the attachment towards people, and things while carrying on the day-to-day work. To the uninitiated observer it might seem as if the Karma Yogi is not different from the ordinary householder. But his dedication to the divine is manifest in everything he does. Perhaps one of the greatest Karma Yogis of all time was Swami Vivekananda who was chosen by his Guru to carry the flame of Vedanta to the western world. He lived among people enjoying the good life, eating and participating in the life of the ordinary human being. His extraversion enabled him to convey the message of Vedanta to the whole of humanity. He did not choose to veil his obvious charisma and physical handsomeness in his essays into the world of people. In one of his lecture programmes, a lady even accused him of hypnotising his audience by his intellect and charm. In reply he said that he was de-hypnotising people from their ignorance of the ultimate reality. While in India and in the West he has been known to enjoy the good life. He was not one who was reticent to ask for food that he relished. This was not understood by the common people who sometimes resented his seeming indulgence in the delights of the flesh. It has been said that his Guru gave him a special dispensation for his food preferences. Still he remained unsullied by the things of the flesh. Swamiji was able to go into Nirvikalpa Samadhi at specified times of his choosing sometimes remaining in that state for long periods of time. His disciples and associates were often dismayed when he would not respond to attempts to awaken him. Swamiji had left specific instructions to those around him as to how he could be brought back to the land of the living by certain methods including massage. One could classify Swamiji as an extraverted person because of his seeming socialising tendency and reliance on objectivity as against the ultimate Pratyahara of the Sanyasi. However, Swamiji was one of those special human beings who defy classification into the dichotomy we have discussed above.

One of the remarkable things about the Karma Sanyasi and also of the Karma Yogi is his capacity to discard the body at the time of his choosing. It is common knowledge that Jesus knew when the time of his departure from this world was due. However he could never persuade his disciples and his associates about this. Some statements that he made while he walked this earth are significant. He said: "My time is not yet come" in the early days of his ministry. During the last days of his life among the people of this earth he clearly indicated the time that he was to leave the body and the way in which it was going to be accomplished. Ramakrishna Paramahansa, Ramana Maharishi and Swamiji Vivekananda were all able to tell those around them the way in which they would leave the body. There are many other Sanyasis and Karma Yogis who have had this preknowledge about these phenomena, but time and space dictate that I cannot deal with their lives here.

Paradise Lost And Regained

Some people do not believe the story of the Creation of man described in Genesis, the first book of the Holy Bible. Others there are, who swear by it. But here is the story. After having created heaven and earth and all the living things therein, God said: "Let us make man in our image, after our likeness: and let them have dominion over the fish of the sea and over the fowl of the air, and over the cattle and over all the earth, and over every creeping thing that creepeth upon the earth." So the Lord God fashioned man out of the dust of the ground and breathed into his nostrils the breath of life and man became a living soul. God then put man in the Garden of Eden, His most beautiful piece of creation. Not only were the flora and fauna beautiful, but there was also an ingenious arrangement whereby a mist went up from the earth and watered the whole garden. In other ways too the Garden of Eden was special because it had two unusual trees growing in it, one the Tree of Life and the other The Tree of knowledge of good and evil. God said to the man that he could eat of the fruit of any of the trees of the garden except that from the Tree of Knowledge. He made it plain to man that if he did eat the fruit of that tree, he would surely die. Otherwise, Adam the first man had free run of the whole garden. He even named the flora and fauna. It is not clear why God thought Adam could be lonely. However, He made a deep sleep to come over him. He took out one of his ribs, clothed it with flesh and made the first woman whom Adam named Eve. That is why in all Christian weddings it is customary for the celebrant to say: "Therefore shall a man leave his father and his mother, and shall cleave unto his wife; and they shall be one flesh." The most significant aspect of the life of the couple was they were both naked, the man and his wife, and they were not ashamed.

Reading further, the first mention of the serpent occurs. Of all God's creation, the serpent was the most subtle. It is rather significant that the serpent approached Eve rather than Adam, saying to her that if she ate of the fruit of the Tree of Knowledge, she would certainly not die, as God had said. On the other hand her eyes would be opened and she would be as the Gods, knowing good and evil. Eve did not need much persuasion and she took of the forbidden fruit, gave it also to Adam and they both ate. Instantly their eyes were opened and the first thing they realised was that they were naked. In other words, their libido was awakened. And among other things, they had lost their precious innocence. Later when they heard the voice of God calling them for the customary walk in the Garden, they hid themselves. When God enquired further, Adam said that he had hidden himself because he was naked. Not only that he put the blame on Eve saying; "The woman thou gavest to be with me, she gave me of the fruit of the tree, and I did eat." Even the first man was quick to blame his transgressions on his woman companion, which continues to this day!

God put a curse on the serpent in that it would have to creep along without any legs. Moreover there would be enmity between the woman and the serpent for all generations to come. To the woman God said that because of her disobedience she would bring forth her children with great pain and suffering. God said to Adam: "Cursed is the ground for thy sake, in sorrow shalt thou eat of it all the days of thy life; thorns and thistles shall it bring forth to thee. In the sweat of thy face shalt thou eat bread until thou return to the ground; for out of it wast thou taken." Then God drove the man and woman out of the Garden of Eden and put an Angel with a fiery sword to guard the entrance to the Garden lest man enter it and eat the fruit of the tree of life.

There are many questions, which arise from this story. Why would God need the company of man, after having spent aeons by Himself? If God made man in his own image, whence did the disobedience come? Could not God in his omniscience have known that it would be too much for man if temptation were put in his way? Why have the Tree of Knowledge of Good and Evil in that garden if man were forbidden to touch its fruit? These questions will remain till the end of time to exercise the minds of people.

According to the Kundalini theory, when God first made man, the Serpent Power was concentrated on the Sahasrara Chakra at the crown of the head. The fall of man represented the dispersal of Kundalini over the whole body especially the viscera. Some Yogis have said that at that stage the Kundalini became like an inverted tree with its roots firmly embedded in the Sahasrara Chakra and the branches growing downwards to the Muladhara Chakra. The viscera being the location of the sensual appetites, the libido was also awakened in the process. But one thing has not been explained. Why did the Kundalini spread downwards in the first place and make man a sensual being?

The Karma Theory offers the fallen man an opportunity to regain the Paradise he had lost. The Atman, which is inherent in every human being, is already pure and perfect having been made in the image of God. The impurity and ignorance are not *in* the Atman but surrounding it as encrustations, preventing its light from illuminating the life of man. Like a brilliant diamond that has fallen in the mire, the dirt prevents its lustre from being seen. Unfortunately, or fortunately as some learned people believe, the human being in this life does not remember all the mistakes he has made in past lives or the crimes he had committed. It is only between one birth and the next that he has access to the memory of all his past deeds. At this stage no extraneous force or entity intervenes in his Karmic choices. The Atman chooses for itself the kind of birth it is going to have, the suffering or pleasures it wishes to encounter and the extent to which the encrustations shall be removed in that particular birth. There is also the possibility that the Grace of God can wash the Atman clean of all encrustations. Anyhow the end product is the acquisition of two essential aspects of inner Knowledge, "aham brahmasmi" and "tat tvam asi" translated respectively as I am Brahman and That thou art, both referring to the divinity of man. At this stage, the individual Atman is ready to merge with the Godhead.

The Christians have another recourse to the regaining of the Paradise, which Adam and Eve literally threw away. Jesus the Christ was born to help man towards this end. He acquired a human body and allowed this body to be tortured and killed, taking upon himself the sins of the whole world. Many Christians mistakenly speak of the death of Jesus. He, being God himself, could not have died. (It has to be understood that in this context, death for anyone only means the separation of the immortal soul from the body. In that sense no one dies.) The body that Jesus took on died and was replaced by another resplendent one. This vicarious sacrifice that Jesus undertook is very hard to understand. However preachers continue to harangue congregations from pulpit to pulpit. But do they understand this mystery? I should say not. I think we have to go to the norms and rituals of Jewish culture to have an inkling of what it is all about. Once a year, it was customary for the Jews to select a goat without any blemishes, which the Rabbi would invest with all the sins of the people, after which it would be driven into the harsh wilderness to perish. It was hoped that by this means atonement would be achieved. The people would then be free of their sins.

The concept of the Scapegoat as we know it today was derived from this important ritual. Every culture has its scapegoat. The institution of Apartheid was based on this concept and it worked for the White people magnificently. Whenever anything went wrong the black people could be blamed. In Australia, the Aboriginal people have been scapegoats for a couple of centuries and continue to be so to this day. Speaking of vicarious sacrifices, in the indigenous law of the Aboriginal people if for some reason the person who had committed a crime was not available, the law would be fulfilled adequately if another person were willing to suffer the punishment. Many an innocent person has thus volunteered to be speared, demonstrating the principle of vicarious atonement.

Indians have always known that physical suffering and deformities could be transferred from one person to another especially at the behest of an evolved man. Thus Babaji and Sri Ramakrishna Paramahansa are two of the well-known holy men who took upon themselves the diseases of their disciples, suffering intensely for a predetermined period. It is a historical fact that when Prince Humayun was seriously ill, his father the Emperor Babar took upon himself the illness of his son and he died in the process, while Humayun lived. In so far as Hindu mythology is concerned there are innumerable stories of such transference of physical impediments including old age, from person to person.

If physical characteristics could be transferred, it stands to reason it should also be possible for an evolved person to take upon himself the sins of others, which is what Jesus the Christ has done. However, it is incumbent on the erstwhile sinner not to commit the same mistakes again. Whenever Jesus forgave the sins of someone, He always said: "Go and sin no more."

Although the human being can regain the Paradise he had once lost, it is perhaps impossible for him to get back the innocence that he once had. There is only one way in which this could be done. Jesus called a little child unto him, and set him in the midst of them. And He said, "Verily I say unto you, except ye be converted, and become as little children, ye shall not enter into the kingdom of heaven."

Epilogue

All things good or bad must come to an end sometime or the other. Existential psychology teaches us that the interpretation that an experiencer places on events determines the meaning that is inherent in them. Having perused the book, the reader may have come across many ways in which a therapist works with clients having many different types of problems in life. He/she may have realised that perhaps the techniques are not the most significant measures but the attitudes of the client and the therapist towards them. For an existentialist therapist the process of treatment is as exciting as it is for the client. Another important aspect that has to be realised is that in all kinds of existential treatments, a directive approach is adopted as against the non-directive approach of most psychotherapies. This has a direct relationship to Indian approaches to spirituality in which the Guru or the preceptor sets out clearly the path to be followed by the disciple. The same principle applies to existential therapy also. Although the therapist might set out the directions to be followed and indicate to the client the path to take, in the final analysis it is up to the latter to take this advice. In this way the freedom of will of the client is respected. Take for example the Paradoxical Intention one of the crucial pillars of Logotherapy. Not only does the therapist encourage the client to act in specific ways which may sometimes be intensely uncomfortable to follow, he gently nudges the client to acquiesce. This has a distinct flavour of the Christian approach to life in general.

From the point of view of the therapist also, another important measure has to be looked at. This is the concept of attachment the therapist might develop towards the client. This author does not believe in clinical detachment nor does he believe in holding on to the client when all the parameters indicate that the relationship has to come to an end. Again this relates to the Christian concept of *Agape* which means a comprehensive love relationship without a cloying attachment. The Vedanta philosophy also enjoins the highest form of love as one that embraces the whole of humanity. In the life of Jesus this has been demonstrated times without number. He loved everyone but showed no excessive attachment to anyone in particular.

I have one request to make to the reader. Do not be discouraged if after one reading things are a bit hazy. Please go back again and make another attempt.

0-595-29438-3

www.ingramcontent.com/pod-product-compliance
Lightning Source LLC
Chambersburg PA
CBHW021548290526
45784CB00016B/945